HINDOO AND MAHOMEDAN BUILDINGS.

VIEWS IN India, China AND ON THE SHORES OF THE Red Sea

Drawn by D. Roberts. Eng. by permission from Capt. Grindlay's Work 8vo. coloured. Engraved and PRINTED IN OIL COLOURS by G. Baxter, 29, King Square

HINDOO AND MAHOMEDAN BUILDINGS.

EDIFICES INDIENS ET MAHOMETANS. HINDOOSTANISCHE UND MAHOMEDANISCHE GEBAUDE.

FISHER & Co. LONDON, 1835.

VIEWS IN India, China AND ON THE SHORES OF THE Red Sea

DRAWN BY
PROUT, STANFIELD, CATTERMOLE,
PURSER, COX, AUSTEN, & C.

FROM ORIGINAL SKETCHES BY
COMMANDER ROBERT ELLIOTT

WITH DESCRIPTIONS BY
EMMA ROBERTS

VOLUME I-II

Gian Publishing House

29/6 SHAKTI NAGAR · DELHI-110007 · INDIA

GIAN PUBLISHING HOUSE
PUBLISHERS OF BOOKS ON HUMAN CIVILIZATION
29/6 SHAKTI NAGAR, DELHI-110007, INDIA

First Indian Reprint, 1986

Printed at Goyal Offset Printers, Delhi-110035
and published by Smt. Gayatri Garg
for Gian Publishing House, Delhi-110007

VIEWS IN

INDIA.

CHINA,

AND ON

THE SHORES OF THE RED SEA;

DRAWN BY

PROUT, STANFIELD, CATTERMOLE, PURSER, COX, AUSTEN, &c.

FROM ORIGINAL SKETCHES

BY

COMMANDER ROBERT ELLIOTT, R. N.

WITH

DESCRIPTIONS BY EMMA ROBERTS.

VOL. I.

PREFACE.

THE interest which our splendid territories in the East are so justly calculated to excite, has been hitherto stifled by the overwhelming nature of the studies supposed to be necessary to the attainment of a very moderate degree of knowledge relative to their history, their antiquities, their religious creeds, and the modes and manners of their various inhabitants.

The fields of Oriental literature, until very lately, have been almost exclusively occupied by the researches of learned men, whose lucubrations, though of the highest value, are not adapted to the general reader; while a vast quantity of information, of a more popular kind, remains locked up in expensive quartos, and is consequently inaccessible to a large portion of the community. The attempt, therefore, to remove some of the difficulties attendant upon an acquaintance with the numerous objects of interest and attention with which our Indian possessions abound; will doubtless prove acceptable to all inquiring minds; and though the plan of the present work does not admit of any detailed account of the various cities and provinces illustrated in the accompanying engravings, nothing has been omitted which the limits would allow, calculated to excite interest, and to induce the reader to enter more deeply into the study of Indian history.

Many of the scenes described in the following pages are familiar to the writer; and she has spared no pains in procuring information from the most authentic sources, concerning places which she had no opportunity of visiting in person. It has not always been possible to give the exact measurements or the dates of the buildings which embellish the splendid landscapes of Hindostan; and where these are wanting, the Author has endeavoured to invest the subject with an interest of a different nature, by the introduction of characteristic traits of the native inhabitants of the neighbourhood, the political history of the country, or descriptions of its scenery and natural productions.

In glancing over the engravings illustrative of a land almost unknown to those who have become its undisputed rulers, no eye can fail to be struck with the architectural splendours of its palaces, its temples, and its tombs. Art and nature have been equally prodigal in the embellishments of a soil rich in foliage, fruit, and flower, teeming with animal life, and watered by many a noble stream, whose glittering currents give fertility to the laughing plains, and valleys thick with corn.

The wild shores of the Red Sea, the populous rivers of China, and the gem-like isles of the Eastern archipelago, have furnished subjects for a work which embraces a very large and interesting portion of Asia; and amid the information which has been collected concerning these remote scenes, will be found extracts from the translation of a Persian MS., and the latest descriptions of Canton, taken from a periodical published in China, of which very few copies have found their way into this country. The author gladly avails herself of the opportunity afforded her to offer her thanks to those who have so kindly aided her researches. She feels most particularly indebted to George Bennett, Esq., author of "Wanderings in New South Wales," and to Sir Alexander Johnstone, and the Members of the Asiatic Society, for the access granted to the library of their establishment, and for permission to make use of some very valuable MSS., especially one relative to the city of Bejapore.

CONTENTS OF VOL. I.

* HINDOO AND MAHOMEDAN BUILDINGS.—In the Frontispiece it is intended to give some of the leading characteristics of the sacred architecture of India. The spectator is supposed to stand in the porch of a Hindoo temple, the proportions and details of which are strictly copied from a very ancient shrine, dedicated to Mahades, of extraordinary richness, still existing at Moondheyra, in the north-west of Guzerat, near the ancient Nehrwala, now called Puttun, or "The City."

† SCENE IN BUNDELKHUND.—The Vignette Engraving affords a very accurate representation of the general nature of the scenery in Bundelkhund, which, for the most part, is broken into deep defiles and ravines, the hills on either side being table-land, and the greater portion crowned with some edifice,—a temple, a tomb, or the remains of a fortress.

AURUNGZEBE'S MOSQUE, AT BENARES.

ILLUSTRATIONS

OF

INDIA,

CHINA, AND THE SHORES OF THE RED SEA.

BENARES.

In ascending the Ganges, the first indication given to the anxious stranger of his approach to the holy city, is afforded by those lofty minarets which tower above the dense mass of buildings, spread in picturesque confusion, along the curved margin of the river, to the distance of nearly five miles. Cold indeed must be the heart which does not glow as the gorgeous panorama discloses itself, and temple, and tower, long pillared arcade, broad ghaut, and balustraded terrace, come forth in full relief, interspersed with the rich dark green foliage of the peepul, the tamarind, and the banian; and, garlanded at intervals with lustrous flowers, peeping through the interstices of highly sculptured buildings, bright tenants of some blooming garden sequestered amid their spacious courts.

Few cities, however splendid, present so great a variety of attractive objects as Benares. The absence of all regular plan, the great diversity of the architecture, the mixture of the stern and solemn with the light and fantastic, give a grotesque appearance to some portions of the scene; but the effect of the whole is magnificent, and many of the details are of almost inconceivable beauty.

The ghauts, or landing places, broad flights of steps descending into the river, are the only quays, if such they may be called, which the city possesses: the buildings for the most part project into the water, although it is thirty feet below the level of the bank, and the whole line, from sunrise, until long after sunset, is swarming with busy multitudes engaged in various occupations. The ghauts are crowded with people, some lading or unlading the numerous native vessels which convey merchandise to and from this grand mart for the commerce of Hindoostan Proper; others drawing water, performing their ablutions, or engaged in prayer; for, notwithstanding the multiplicity of the temples, the religious worship of the Hindoo is performed in the open air.

Although the rooted hatred entertained by the followers of the prophet, against every species of idolatry, prompted them to promulgate their own creed by fire and sword, wheresoever their victorious armies penetrated, the desecration of the holy city was not effected until the reign of Aurungzebe. The emperor being determined to humble the boast of the Brahmins, levelled one of their most ancient and venerated pagodas to the ground, and erected a mosque on its site, whose slender spires, springing up into the golden expanse above, seem to touch the skies. In a city so crowded with splendid architectural objects, it required some bold and happy design, to produce a building which should eclipse them all; and this has certainly been effected by the minarets, which attract and arrest the gazer's eye from every point.

Previous to the erection of these graceful trophies of the Moghul conquest of Hindoostan, the Brahmins pretended that their city could not be effected by any of the changes and revolutions which distracted the world, of which it formed no part, being the creation of Siva after the curse had gone forth which brought sin and sorrow upon earth, and upheld by the point of his trident. The priesthood have been obliged to abate some of their lofty pretensions, since Moslem temples have been raised beside the shrines of their deities' and blood, not required for sacrifice, has been, and continues to be shed within the precincts of the city.

The Moosulman inhabitants do not choose to relinquish their *kababs*, in consideration for the religious scruples of their Hindoo neighbours, and kill and eat without ceremony. They have established butchers' shops in some of the principal thoroughfares, which display, upon long skewers, those lean morsels of meat, the most esteemed roasts of an Asiatic board, but which, previous to their removal to the *Bur wachee khana*, cook room, furnish a delicious regale to some millions of blue-bottle flies. Formerly the slaughter of an animal by any hand save that of the priest, and for any purpose excepting that of religious sacrifice, would have occasioned a revolt in the holy city: but the Brahmins have now been accustomed to see the sacred cow fall a victim to the appetites of their rulers; the neighbouring bazaars are well supplied with both beef and veal, articles of food from which the East India Company's civil and military servants, unwilling to offend the religious prejudices of the natives, for a long period, abstained in this, the strong hold of their superstition.

Although the view of Benares from the river, must be considered the most beautiful and imposing, no correct idea can be formed of this singular city, without penetrating into the interior, threading its mazy labrynths, and taking a bird's-eye-view from some towering height. The ascent of the minarets is usually attempted by those who are not afraid of encountering fatigue. The open cupola, or lanthorn, at the top, is gained by a narrow, but not very inconvenient stair, but as, with the want of precaution common to all classes of Asiatics, the apertures for the admission of light and air, are left totally unguarded, it is only those who possess strong heads and well-strung nerves, who can look down through these dangerous apertures, without encountering a very painful degree of dizziness and tremor.

After winding through lanes and alleys, so narrow that a single individual must be jostled by every person he meets, and where a brahmanee bull, an animal privileged to roam wheresoever he chooses, may block up the passage, and render it impassable during his pleasure, the astonishment is very great, when we perceive that the closeness of the city is chiefly confined to its avenues. Looking down from the minarets, or some other commanding height, upon the city of Benares, as it lies spread out like a map beneath us, we are surprised by the stately gardens and spacious quadrangles occupying the ground between the high buildings which line the narrow streets. Some of these secluded retreats are remarkably beautiful, surrounded by cloisters of stone, decorated with a profusion of florid ornaments, and flanked by some high tower, whence the most delightful prospect imaginable may be obtained of the adjacent country, with its fertile plains, umbrageous woods, and ever-shining river. Others, smaller, are laid out in parterres of flowers, with a fountain playing in the centre, and all are tenanted by numerous birds of the brightest and most resplendent plumage, flocks of every variety of the pigeon and the dove common to the plains, blue jays, yellow-breasted sparrows, and whole battalions of ring-necked paroquets, with their brilliant feathers gleaming like emeralds in the sun, as they skim along, soaring far above the mango trees which bear their nests, yet seldom overtopping the crowning pinnacle of the minaret, whence the spectator surveys the singular and beautiful objects revealed to his admiring gaze.

At a short distance from the minarets,to the left, the house of the Peishwa, a Mahratta prince of great wealth, is visible in the accompanying plate, towering above all the other buildings; it is seven stories in height, and from the terrace on its roof, which is surrounded by a parapet breast high, a prospect as extensive as that from the minarets, may be obtained.

It is no uncommon circumstance, for the princes and nobles of Hindoostan, whose possessions lie at a considerable distance, to build or purchase a residence in the holy city, to which they may repair during the celebration of particular festivals, and where they are anxious, when worn out by the cares of state and the deceitfulness of the world, to spend their last days. Those who die at Benares, in the favour of the Brahmins, are assured of immediate absorption into the divine essence; nor is this privilege confined to any sect or caste; such is the sanctity of the place, that persons who have committed the most frightful crimes, or have ever been convicted of that worst species of sacrilege, eating beef, may secure a glorious immortality, by yielding up their spirit in this hallowed spot, provided always that they have been charitable to the Brahmins.

Though there is no garden or pleasure-ground attached to the Peishwa's residence, the building affords a very fair specimen of the habitations of wealthy Hindoos. There are outer windows only on one side next the street, which contains seven large apartments, rising over each other; the rest of the chambers open upon covered galleries, surrounding three sides of a small court, and the communication from story to story is very curious. A single flight of stairs leads from the lower to the upper apartment, which must be crossed before the next flight can be gained; a mode of constructing a staircase which is often seen in native buildings in India, and which suits well with the jealous precautions formerly necessary in the unsettled state of the country. Some of the apartments are furnished with bedsteads peculiar to the Mahrattas, a platform of polished wood, slightly curved, suspended from the ceiling at an easy distance from the ground: the panels and pillars of these rooms are of carved wood, and their decorations were composed of rich carpets, and silver vessels, very splendidly wrought.

HINDOO TEMPLE,—BENARES.

To build a temple, plant a tree, or dig a well, are benefits to posterity which are strictly enjoined to the wealthy classes of society, by the religious precepts both of the Moslem and the Hindoo; but as there is no especial clause to ensure the repair of any edifice, the ravages of the climate, and the devastations of time, are permitted to go on without any attempt to arrest the progress of destruction. Prevention and cure are held in equal disdain by the natives of India. It is no uncommon thing to see two or three of the lower steps of some splendid ghaut, separated by a couple of feet from the upper flight, which is thus rendered useless; but nobody dreams of restoration, and, should there be any rich person in the neighbourhood desirous of dying in the odour of sanctity, instead of repairing the dilapidations, he will construct another ghaut at a little distance. In the event of his decease before the completion of his purpose, there will not be the slightest chance of its being finished by his heirs or assigns. Every one is anxious to get a *burra nam* (great name) for himself, and public spirit does not extend to the sacrifice of personal ambition to general utility.

The history of the pagoda in the plate before us, is that of many other buildings of equal beauty in India; the foundation has been suffered to wear away, and the erections, which it should have supported, have fallen into the water. The antiquity of this temple is shewn by the pointed mitre-like dome which crowns each tower, the round flattened cupola not having been introduced into Hindoo architecture, until after the Moghul conquest. It is now rather difficult to distinguish at a short distance, the small mhut of the worshippers of Brahma, from the equally diminutive mosque of the true believers.

At an early hour in the morning, the officiating priests of the different temples of Benares are all astir: some repeat passages from the vedas, for the edification of those who bring holy water from the Ganges, to pour upon the images, or who come to make offerings at the shrines, while others scatter flowers around. Baskets filled with floral treasures, magnificent in size and splendid in hue, are offered for sale at the gates of the pagodas, and the pavements are literally strewed with large red, white, and yellow blossoms, which would form the most brilliant carpet in the world, were it not for the constant puddle occasioned by the streams of water pouring down on all sides.

In some of the courts of the principal pagodas, we found a fat Brahmanee bull established. These pampered and petted creatures are suffered to roam at large through the

HINDOO TEMPLE. — BENARES.

bazaars, where they help themselves very plentifully to the grain or vegetables which lie temptingly exposed in open baskets within their reach. No one is permitted to molest them, and, unless under very peculiar circumstances, few would be desirous to dispute the road with an animal protected by the law, as well as by his own strength. I have seen one of these bulls butting at a tree in such a furious manner, as to give me reason to suppose that there would be great danger in a personal encounter, but, during my residence in India, I never heard of loss of life occasioned by an attack from any one, amid the numbers which infest the neighbourhood of a Hindoo city or village. Sometimes they will lie down across a street, and, grown lazy by high feeding, refuse to rise. In this predicament, a Hindoo has no alternative; he must wait patiently until the sacred beast shall move of his own accord: but Christians and Moosulmans have a more summary way of settling the matter; they try the effect of blows, and the lower classes of both religions, if the darkness of the night will afford them an opportunity, will quietly lead the animal away to some convenient place, where they soon give him the *coup de grace*, and fare sumptuously on his remains.

Notwithstanding the sacred character of the whole species, the bulls taken under the protection of the priesthood are alone exempt from mal-treatment. A Hindoo, though he would not massacre an ox or a cow for the world, has no objection to starve or overwork it; his tenderness to animals only extends to a refusal to take their lives, and a disinclination to injure them by any act of mere wanton cruelty. One or two sects are, however, exceedingly scrupulous, and it is to these that sick flies are indebted for their hospitals.

All the animals belonging to the city of Benares, or any village under the exclusive dominion of the Hindoo priesthood, are secure from violence; but there are a few peculiarly sacred, which go under the name of Brahmanee. The bulls reared in the temples have been already mentioned; there are also Brahmanee ducks, and Brahmanee lizards: why the latter have attained their sanctity I never heard, but there is an interesting legend attached to the feathered protegès. They are supposed to be the souls of human delinquents transmigrated into the bodies of these animals, and punished by an extraordinary affection for each other, which renders separation a source of the most poignant anguish. The male and female, it is said, are compelled by a mysterious power, to part at sunset; they fly on the opposite sides of the river, each supposing that its mate has voluntarily abandoned the nest, and imploring the truant to return by loud and piercing cries. The pitiable condition of these mourners has excited the compassion of the benevolent Brahmins, who have thrown the ægis of their name over unfortunate beings cursed by the gods.

In an account of the temples of Benares, some notice of the crowds of beggars, of every description, which block up the avenues to pagodas in peculiar request, must not be omitted. Many of these mendicants are of the most hideous description—maimed cripples, distorted by accident, or the religious inflictions by which they acquire the reputation of extraordinary sanctity. Numbers have no covering whatsoever, except filth and chalk, their long beards and matted hair; but there are others sturdy, well clad, and in excellent case, beggars by vocation, who would esteem themselves degraded, should they endeavour to obtain a subsistence by any other means. I have seen one of these sleek suppliants absolutely worry the servants of our establishment out of a portion of the grain intended for their own meal, using the most violent gesticulations in enforcing their petition, and weeping bitterly at a refusal.

Some of the temples maintain a set of dancing girls, who reside in apartments appropriated to their use, belonging to the establishment—attending at religious processions, and performing at all the festivals. The conduct of these ladies is not quite immaculate; but they are not the less esteemed on that account, since theirs is a sacred calling: any crime whatsoever may be perpetrated in India, under the cloak of religion; and though the British government persists in punishing those which come under the cognizance of the established law, a great deal is going on, over which it can have no control.

SHUHUR,—JEYPORE.

Jeypore, a Rajpoot state, and one of the central provinces of India, although not boasting the picturesque beauty and abundant fertility of some of its neighbours, is rich in objects of curiosity, both natural and artificial. The fortress of Shuhur, rising boldly on a rocky ledge, one of those picturesque eminences which intersect the plains of India, varying their monotony, presents an object of feudal grandeur, which transports the European stranger back to the ages of chivalry.

Colonel Tod, in his admirable work upon Rajasthan, has traced the strong resemblance between the institutions of the northern nations, and those of the warlike states of India, and we cannot travel through any portion of this interesting country without meeting with some object to call up recollections associated with the crusades, the baronial wars, and the feuds of christian warriors. A horseman clad in chain mail, bearing his vizor up, and armed with shield and lance, mounted on a gallant steed, richly caparisoned, and clattering under the weight of defensive armour, will pass us on the road, like a knight repairing to a tournament. If we meet a chief, we find him surrounded by spearmen, and we rarely encounter fire-arms of more modern construction than those which succeeded the hand cannon, the matchlock, and arquebus.

The distinguishing title of the children of the soil, "the mild Hindoo," so long supposed to be characteristic of all the tribes who venerate the cow, and refuse to shed the blood of animals; now that we have become more extensively acquainted with the country, is discovered to be wholly confined to the stunted, timorous race found in Bengal and a few other districts on the coast. The inhabitants of the upper and central provinces have much more of the lion than the lamb in their composition; and the Rajpoots, especially, whose trade is war, make some of the finest soldiers in the world. The Bengal army, so called in consequence of the name of the presidency to which it is attached, does not recruit its ranks in the province from which it takes its appellation, but is chiefly composed of daring spirits from Oude, Pytauns of high blood, and the descendants of a race of princes, the warriors of Rajasthan.

SHUHUR, — JEYPORE.

The instant that we pass the boundaries of Bengal, we are struck with the change in the stature and appearance of the population. Tall athletic men, bearing a martial air, succeed to the diminutive and obsequious Bengalee. The natives of the Upper Provinces are altogether a finer race, morally as well as physically: they not only make better soldiers, but better servants; they are, generally speaking, more active and trustworthy, and more susceptible of generous treatment: and they may be depended upon with confidence in any emergence, for, where they are attached, they will stand by their employers to the last, and defend them at the hazard of their lives.

As we penetrate farther into the heart of India, we meet with stronger indications of the military spirit which pervades the country. Since the fall of Bhurtpore, the expiring effort of the neighbouring states to resist the progress of British ascendance, the land has been at peace; but it is easy to perceive that the sword, though no longer drawn, has not been laid aside. The cities and villages are still provided with those primitive defences, considered efficient in a country in which the art of war has not progressed as in Europe, or been reduced to a science; and the numerous fortresses crowning many a desert height, still bristle with spears, and reflect the sun's beams from targets and crested helms. The province of Jeypore, with its arid wastes and toppling sand-hills, seems to be the fit retreat of the storm fiend, whose withering breath is poured in scorching blasts over the plains of Hindoostan. Though from the parched and apparently exhausted soil, crops are produced in extraordinary abundance, so fertilizing are the rains, so exuberantly fruitful the earth of these sunny realms, during many months of the year, Jeypore exhibits a howling wilderness. Yet still it is not destitute of vegetation. When the exhausted travelier sinks down, as the deceptious hope which pointed to lakes and pools, receding as he advances, leaves him to all the horrors of thirst, he finds a welcome solace and relief in those gigantic water-melons, which rise amid the sand, and come to perfection in the hottest and driest seasons.

In the rocky parts of Jeypore, precious stones of considerable value are procured at little trouble and expense; the garnets are particularly beautiful, and amethysts and other gems sell at comparatively low prices. The capital of the province is a grand mart for pearls: occasionally great bargains may be obtained of this chaste gem; the common cost is somewhat less than in places more remote from the commerce of Persia: a pearl of the size of an ordinary pea, which at Delhi is sold for twenty rupees, (two pounds,) may be had for seventeen at Jeypore. The political influence which is still retained by females, in provinces which have never been thoroughly subjugated to the dominion of the jealous Moghuls, is strikingly manifested in the somewhat romantic history of the young sovereign of Jeypore. It it well known that he is a surreptitious child, placed upon the throne by the intrigues of the clever and artful woman who calls herself his mother. She was the favourite of the late Rajah; and at his death being anxious to uphold the share which she had obtained in the government of the country, imposed the offspring of one of her domestics as her own. The Rajah died childless; but this lady, pretending to be in the way to become a mother, produced an heir to the throne; and, aided by the influence of a man of high rank and great popularity, contrived to get herself appointed to the regency, with the title of Maha Ranee. As soon as it was practicable, she introduced the child at a feast, at which a large proportion of the nobles were assembled; and after they had eaten rice with him, became quite assured that the imposture, if discovered, never would be made the subject of public discussion. The real mother of the infant, it appeared, was a sweeper, a class held in the utmost abhorrence by the high-born Hindoos, who would consider themselves polluted if these outcasts only touched the hems of their garments. Had the true parentage of the young prince been revealed, many heads of houses must have shared in his degradation. All who had dipped their hands in the same dish with him, would have lost caste; and their silence and co-operation were effectually secured by so important a stake. Though many perons, discontented at the ascendance gained by this ambitious woman, were ripe and ready for war, the times were not favourable for an outbreak; the fortunate plebeian is firmly seated on his throne, and the country is as much settled as it can be; having lost its independence, yet suffered by the policy imposed on the local powers by the British authorities at home, to be harassed by disorder and misrule. The mild and wise measures, the equal distribution of justice, and respect of property, characterizing the Christian government of India, have reconciled all the provinces enjoying these inestimable benefits, to its dominion; but while the yoke of a conqueror is severely felt in the constrained obedience to tyrants of their own name and nation, the miserable inhabitants of the central provinces are deprived of every advantage arising from our power in the East.

SEVEN-STORIED PALACE,—BEJAPORE.

Wheresoever the Moghuls planted their victorious banners, and assumed dominion, however brief, over the conquered soil, they have left behind them trophies of their power and magnificence, of the most imposing and attractive nature. The buildings of this highly-refined and luxurious people still in existence throughout the scenes of their conquests in Hindostan, that bright and gem-fraught land, tempting so many venturous swords, are not more distinguished for the splendour and elegance of their designs, than for the surpassing beauty of the workmanship. What pomp of pillars and porticos, arched gateways, cupolas, and pinnacled minars, is displayed in the temples, tombs, and palaces reared by their hands! what fret-work and tracery, what lavish ornaments of carved and sculptured stone! and how beautifully do these towers and domes, cloistered quadrangles, and terraced heights, harmonize with the rich foliage of the tamarind, intruding into the deserted courts and the glassy waters of the tanks or jheels beside them!

The loneliness which now surrounds buildings once filled with the retinue of haughty satraps, and redolent with sounds of gladness, is almost of an awful character: desolate creatures inhabit the chambers where beauty held her court, and the wolf and the jackal bay the moon, unscared, in gardens formerly sacred to feminine recreation, the secure asylum of those domestic favourites which woman delights to cherish.

PALACE OF THE SEVEN STORIES, — BEEJAPORE

TIGER ISLAND.

The European traveller who pitches his tent amid these proud reliques, himself the *burra saib,* the great personage of the scene, surveys, with feelings allied to pain, the magnificent yet sad memorials of fallen grandeur. If visiting them on military duty, he is engaged in an inglorious contest with thieves and vagabonds, whose lawless propensities frequently compel the government to send a detachment of sepoys against them.

The Moslem inhabitants of the city of Bejapore are poor and few. In districts remote from the capital of the Moghul empire, there is little save the remains of palaces, fortresses, and mosques, to indicate the invasion of intolerant conquerors, who obliged those whom they compelled to submit to their dominion, to adopt their creed also. In some places nameless tombs are all that still exist, to shew that the followers of the prophet planted their victorious standard in the midst of a heathen nation. Numbers who embraced the religion of their rulers, have relapsed into idolatry; and the remnant who still turn their faces towards Mecca to pray, have so completely degenerated, and are so strongly addicted to the superstitions of their Hindoo associates, as to be scarcely worthy of the name of Moslems.

The only natives in the neighbourhood of Bejapore, whose appearance can in any degree assimilate with the military splendour of its remains, are the Mahrattas. When those graceful horsemen, clad in wild yet splendid attire, and mounted upon fiery coursers, caracole beneath the walls, somewhat of the martial pageantry of by-gone days returns upon the eye. These men ride with almost miraculous skill, and their charge forms one of the most striking evolutions performed by cavalry. The battalion commences its career in a line two deep, at a brisk canter, which changes into a gallop as it advances; suddenly the files open out, scattering "like a broken string of pearls," each man waving his sword, and uttering a shrill cry, plunges on the object of his attack with maddening vehemence; but while the charge is thus apparently made at random, every man and horse are under the strictest control; at the wildest and most infuriated moment, every warrior will rein up his steed, throwing it upon its haunches, and remaining immoveable until the command be given to charge again.

TIGER ISLAND.

It is much to be regretted that so large a number of intelligent persons should have traded, during a long series of years, to Canton, without adding to the stock of information attained from the narratives of the few travellers who have penetrated the interior of the celestial empire. Our knowledge of the Chinese is chiefly pictorial; we are compelled to glean the history of this curious people from their tea-cups; and while the products of a country, which we are aware must be rich in all the precious commodities, and of prodigious fertility, are disseminated throughout every hamlet in the kingdom, the country itself remains a sort of *terra incognita:* we can form little more than vague guesses concerning the greater portion of it; and even places of note, upon the frontiers, remain still to be minutely described.

Tiger Island is situated within the Canton River, and would, under a more warlike government, prove a sufficient defence from invasion in that channel. It rises in a bluff promontory, and there being a corresponding eminence on the opposite side, which shuts in the river, narrowing it in this part to the width of half-a-mile, skilful engineers might render the passage extremely difficult, if not impracticable. A few batteries have been constructed on the opposite shore, but they are so ill-contrived, as to be utterly contemptible as a fortification, and could not, for a single instant, retard the progress of an armed vessel;—(not a gun could be brought to bear against the Alceste;)—but it has been the policy of the British government to allow the Chinese to play at war; they have not yet been fully taught the inefficiency of their defences against a determined enemy, and, full of self-conceit, they vapour and brag of their military prowess, and flatter themselves that they are secure from foreign invasion.

The Canton river is frequently extremely turbulent, and, in consequence of the difficulty of the navigation, accidents are continually happening to the boats of the Indiamen. The Chinese are always on the look-out, to turn such circumstances to advantage; and when they hasten to the relief of persons in jeopardy, it is invariably with a view to make a profit by it. Before they will rescue a drowning man, they drive hard bargains with him, exacting terms according to the peril of his situation, and the power they possess to turn it to account. They do not appear to have any scruple of conscience about leaving a sufferer to his fate, should he refuse to accede to their exorbitant demands. Such occurrences lower the character of the Chinese to the utmost point of degradation in the opinion of those who witness their inhuman rapacity; but it is unjust to judge a nation by the conduct of a small portion of the community inhabiting the ports, a class of persons who in every country are found to make a prey of all who are cast upon their hospitality. Unfortunately, our scanty knowledge of the tone of morals in the interior, renders us but too apt to form our estimate of the whole from that which comes under our own observation; but it would be quite as safe a criterion to condemn the English nation, on the atrocities committed by the wreckers of the Cornish coast.

Near the entrances of the splendid river which leads to the city, familiarized to every one by its crapes, its varieties of lacquer ware, its ivory, its velvet paper, its fans, and its lanthorns, are numerous islands, called by the Portuguese, the Ladrones, on account of their being infested with bands of pirates, whom the imbecility of the persons at the head of the Chinese government permitted to exist on the very skirts of this sacred empire, which, in their inflated ideas of their own importance, they fancied would be respected by the whole world. These systematic robbers existed solely by plunder, and were for a long time the terror of the adjacent coast, and of the navigators of fishing boats and other small defenceless vessels. It is only lately that they have been entirely extirpated; and the Chinese owe their deliverance from a contemptible, yet harassing enemy, to the skill and conduct of their European allies, and the feuds and rivalries subsisting amid the lawless community, which, when united under one fierce and gifted leader, proved irresistible.

A very spirit-stirring account of a captivity amid these predatory hordes has been

FUTTYPORE SICRI.

lately published by an officer in the India Company's naval service;* we have not the work at hand, to refer to, but retain a vivid recollection of some personal communications made several years ago by this gentleman, who, amongst other interesting circumstances, narrated that he was more than once indebted for his life to the interposition of the chieftain's wife, a woman who subsequently proved herself worthy of a place amidst the heroines of the age. She baffled the attempts of foes from without, and traitors lurking within the bosom of the community, triumphed over treacherous adversaries, gained the respect of open enemies, and succeeded at last in obtaining honourable terms for herself and her followers.

The large vessel in the plate represents a Chinese war-junk, the invention of a barbarous era of naval architecture, and which has sustained no improvement, from the contemplation, by this vain and bigoted people, of the superior craft which commercial speculations bring from Portugal, England, and America. It serves their present purpose, and they depend entirely upon the exclusive system, which has hitherto proved so effective, to preserve their empire inviolate.

FUTTYPORE SICRI.

Futtypore Sicri has not been inaptly termed the Versailles of the Moghul emperors. It lies at the distance of twenty miles from the city of Agra, and was the favourite retreat of Akbar and his descendants. Though now a place of huts and ruins, scantily inhabited by a few poor villagers, its architectural remains are of the most splendid description, equalling, if not surpassing, those of any other province of India.

The gateway, represented in the plate, leading to the mosque attached to the palace of Akbar, is considered the most beautiful specimen of the kind which is to be found in any part of the world: it leads into a quadrangle of magnificent proportions, surrounded on three sides with a fine piazza, the mosque itself being on the fourth, a handsome building, in a plain solid style of architecture, but not quite commensurate with the expectations raised by the splendour of the entrance. The enclosure is about five hundred feet square; its chaste grandeur produces somewhat of a solemn effect, and is associated in the mind with ideas of monastic seclusion and academic study. The whole is kept in excellent repair by the British government, and may, at no very future period, be appropriated to a very noble use, and become the abode of learned men, and the resort of aspiring youth.

Upon entering this spacious area, the visitor is at first struck with the imposing appearance of the whole: absorbed in admiration, he surveys the striking scene with rapt eyes; and it is not until after a considerable period has elapsed, that he can tear himself away from the contemplation, to the examination of the details. Many of these are of exquisite beauty. Facing the entrance are two mausoleums, wrought with all the

* Captain Glasspoole.

care and finish which distinguishes the workmanship of the Moghuls. In the one on the right, several members of the imperial family lie entombed; the other, the shrine of Sheik Soliman is a perfect gem of art, elaborately executed in white marble, of the purest hue and the most delicate sculpture: this holy personage, now esteemed and honoured as a saint, was the friend and counsellor of the great Akbar, and, dying in the odour of sanctity, his shrine is regarded with particular veneration. The emperor was wont, during his campaigns, to leave his wives and children under the care of this trusted minister, and, notwithstanding the extraordinary reputation which his pretensions to piety procured for him, scandal has not scrupled to busy itself with the highly reverenced name, and, by many, Sheik Soliman is supposed to have abused the confidence of his sovereign.

The simple grandeur of the mosque, which is surmounted by three domes, of white marble, and preserves, both in its exterior and interior, a noble plainness, is perhaps more agreeable to the eye than the gorgeous displays which other Moosulmanee temples exhibit; but many persons, impressed with ideas produced by the almost sublime beauty of the lofty tower which forms its portal, are disappointed by the absence of those elaborate ornaments which so profusely adorn the buildings in its neighbourhood. To the eye of taste, however, such accessories are not wanting.

The turret-crowned, embattlemented quadrangle, with its arched cloisters, splendid gateway, and isolated tombs, leave nothing to desire; and strangers quit the scene with regret, returning again and again to feast their eyes upon its calm beauty. To the right of this mosque the remains of Akbar's ruined palace rise amidst courts and terraces, in various stages of decay: the portions which remain entire are particularly interesting; amongst these, the stables of the emperor are worthy of notice; they consist of a spacious street, with a piazza on either side, fifteen feet in width, supported upon handsome pillars, and roofed in with immense slabs of stone, extending from the parapet to the wall.

The residence of Akbar's favourite minister, though upon a small scale, affords a very splendid specimen of Oriental luxury, realizing the ideas of the pavilions and miniature palaces through which we have already wandered in fancy, while perusing the Arabian tales.

In the court of the Zenana, another of these exquisite pieces of workmanship is shewn, by some supposed to have been the bedchamber of one of Akbar's wives, the daughter of the sultan of Constantinople; and by others, a study reserved by the emperor for his own private use. Its remains are exceedingly beautiful; three windows of perforated marble, in the rich tracery which occurs so profusely in all these Moghul buildings, are still entire. The wall has been disfigured by the orders of that arch-hypocrite, Aurungzebe, who, to divert the minds of men from dwelling upon his usurpation of his father's crown, and his relentless persecution of his brothers, affected devotion to religion, and displayed his zeal by the strictest attention to the outward forms and rules prescribed by the Koran. The interior of this pavilion is beautifully carved with trees, clusters of grapes, and birds and beasts, executed with no common degree of skill; but as the strict regulations of Islamism do not permit of such representations, the emperor ordered them to be demolished.

CHINESE PAGODAH,— BETWEEN CANTON & WHAMPOA.

Another of the curiosities consists of a pavement of black and white marble, said to be the relics of an enormous chess-board, on which the kingly satraps played with human beings, personating the different pieces employed in the game so deeply studied by Asiatics. Tradition states, that the great Akbar was somewhat addicted to the occult sciences, and occasionally dabbled in magic rites. A small open pavilion, supported upon four pillars, of very graceful design, is reported to have been the scene of his incantations; but there is no good authority for the support of this opinion.

The audience-chamber of Àkbar, though more curious than beautiful, forms an object of great attraction to the visitors of Futtypore. It is a pavilion of stone, about twenty feet square, surrounded by a gallery of the same materials; the musnud, or throne, not very unlike a pulpit, rises in the centre, and from each of the four sides of the gallery; a narrow bridge, without rails, leads to the place where the emperor, seated in solitary state, received his courtiers, who were not permitted to advance beyond the galleries. It does not appear that the Moghul emperors were accustomed to hold their durbars in similar places; and this singular structure, doubtless owed its creation to a somewhat whimsical fancy on the part of the mighty Akbar.

Though at present very thinly inhabited, the town of Futtypore Sicri is of considerable extent; its mouldering turreted wall is five miles in circumference, but not a tenth portion of the ground which it surrounds is tenanted by human occupants. From the gateway on the road to Agra, a spacious street presents itself, which bears the marks of having once been the residence of wealthy nobles; but the houses on either side are dwindling fast into masses of shapeless ruins. The gate of the mosque before-mentioned forms a sort of beacon to the visitor, though its approach, by a long flight of steps, is rather fatiguing: from the topmost story, a splendid view rewards those who are sufficiently courageous to make the ascent: the eye wanders over a vast extent of country; fields highly cultivated according to the Eastern mode, producing cotton, mustard, rice, and various other kinds of grain; wooded with mango and tamarind groves; watered by broad jheels; and interspersed with a profusion of picturesque buildings, serais, mosques, crumbling palaces, old tombs, and old wells, spread themselves to the north-west to the walls of Bhurtpore, the fortress so famed in the military annals of Hindoostan; while, on the opposite side, the splendid city of Agra, with the snowy dome of the Tâj, a striking object from every direction, closes the scene.

CHINESE PAGODA, BETWEEN CANTON AND WHAMPOA.

This elegant tower stands midway between the city of Canton and Whampoa, which are about twelve miles distant from each other: its graceful style, the loftiness and beauty of its proportions, render it a conspicuous landmark; and the eager eyes of the stranger are delighted to behold the realization of scenes so often pictured to the mind; for who amongst us has not, from childhood, indulged in visions of the bright land associated in the imagination with one continued scene of pageantry? The approach to every foreign country, though differing in minute particulars from our own, cannot fail to strike all, save the most obtuse spectator, with the strangeness of its aspect. But, perhaps, no place in the whole compass of the globe offers such extraordinary and striking novelties as those presented by the grotesque features which characterize the Chinese empire. The dense mass of the population, all busily employed, clad in gaudy bnt uncouth garments, and affording such striking illustrations of the truth of those caricatures of the human face divine, which we have so often laughed at in the groupes depicted upon our china, alike excite our wonder and amazement. The shape of the boats, the appearance of the houses, the floating gardens, and crowded habitations constructed on the water, are all so odd and peculiar, that it is a long time before the mind recovers from its state of pleased surprise: the recognition of some old familiar form, such as we have seen hovering round the India-house in London, or upon a fan or illuminated lanthorn, affords scarcely less gratification than the sight of something perfectly new and undescribed amid the brilliant panorama.

The immense trade carried on by the Chinese, is exemplified by the almost innumerable vessels which, in the precincts of the city of Canton, absolutely choke up a river wider than the Thames at London. Amid the various craft which navigate this swarming stream, the boats employed to convey the contraband goods smuggled into the country by the merchants of the British factory, are the most remarkable. They have a very formidable appearance, and do not depend wholly upon the sufferance of the government, which connives at the violation of its laws. The ships belonging to the dealers in opium are anchored off the island of Lintin, and present the strangest combination of the ship and the counting-house, the warlike and the mercantile, that can be well imagined: here a huge ledger, and there a blunderbuss: in one corner, the last price-current, stuck in the handle of a cutlass; and in another, piles of chests filled with good Spanish dollars; all bespeak the crafty trader, ready to deal in a peaceable way, if such be the wish of those who approach him; or to defend his illegal gains, in case of necessity, against the constituted authorities of the country from whence his wealth is derived. Opium, which is eagerly purchased by all classes of the community, forms the staple commodity of the trade with British India; immense quantities of cotton also are imported; and, in addition to woollen cloths, printed calicoes, and a great variety of other articles, including gems cut and polished by London artisans, English porcelain is now brought to China, though in small quantities, and chiefly as presents. Our extraordinary success in the manufacture of every denomination of this beautiful preparation of clay, has completely ruined the Chinese market: the shops of Calcutta are filled with goods from the Staffordshire potteries; English delf, though brought from so great a distance, being much cheaper, as well as superior, to the common ware made in China, which is heavy and coarse. The exports are now wholly confined to ornamental appendages, in some of which they are still unrivalled. It is said, that a merchant of eminence, having an immense quantity of unsaleable china upon hand, attempted to open a negociation with the prime-minister of the king of England, to whom he offered a handsome bribe, in the expectation of inducing him to procure the abolition of home manufacture of the article he was so anxious to dispose of.

JUMMA MUSJID, — AGRA.

Foreigners are only permitted to visit a particular quarter of the city of Canton, in which there is little to see except the curious figures which inhabit it; and the multitudinous assortment of fancy goods exposed for sale in the shops. No place in the world can be so tempting as a Chinese bazaar; and we must question the wisdom which excludes European ladies from a sight of the irresistible articles, in every ornamental shape, which it contains. The glimpses afforded by the best-stocked warehouses in London, give but a faint idea of the splendour, beauty, ingenuity, and delicacy displayed in the manufactures of this industrious race, in silk, gold, silver, ivory, tortoise-shell, wood, lacquer, and paper. Those white, thick, velvety leaves of the latter, so much in esteem for paintings, both in Europe and Asia, and which, in England, go under the name of rice, is made from the pith of a tree, which in India also is used for many ornamental purposes, though with less skill than by the dexterous fingers of the Chinese. Rice is employed for a very different purpose, it being moulded into a composition resembling stone, of which a great many descriptions of knick-knackery are made, a manufacture in which the Chinese, beyond any other nation, excel: their toys are the most ingenious things imaginable; and though the mechanism by which they are made to move about, is exceedingly clumsy, and liable to get out of order, the imitation of men and animals is so exact, as to put to shame the dolls and horses of the most celebrated makers of London or Paris.

JUMMA MUSJID,— AGRA.

The neglected state of the Jumma Musjid at Agra, its isolated situation, and the exceeding interest and beauty of the adjacent buildings, have renderet it less an object of attention than its intrinsic merits deserve. Many travellers pass through the city without bestowing more then a casual glance upon this splendid mosque, and few are at the trouble to penetrate the interior. It fronts the Delhi gate of the fort, occupying a large open space picturesquely wooded, and partially covered with ruins, which in various stages of decay stretch for miles to the fragments of the old wall, which formerly surounded the city. The architecture of this mosque is extremely grand and solid: it is flanked by octagonal towers, and the walls are strengthened by buttresses. A lofty gateway, surmounted by minarets, leads to the interior, which is rich, chaste, and simple. The Mahommedan religion rejects all extraneous decoration in the adornment of places of public worship, and the lofty cupola'd hall is not decked with those florid ornaments which the tasteful Moghul delights to lavish upon edifices designed for the abodes of the living or the reception of the dead.

The Jumma Musjid is still in good preservation, though it bears marks of greater antiquity than the buildings in its neighbourhood. The time, in all probability, is not far distant, in which its ancient glories shall revive; for the formation of a new presidency at Agra cannot fail to produce very speedy and striking improvements in the appearance of the city. The vast abundance of building-materials, and the facility with which marble and other ornamental stones may be obtained from the central provinces, offers great advantages to those employed in the construction of the numerous edifices which will be necessary for the accommodation of the new inhabitants.

The Delhi gate of the fortress is visible on the right of the plate; a principal entrance of a place of arms, which forms one of the most interesting specimens of fortification which is to be found in India: the defences would not be tenable against artillery of any kind; but it is said to have been a place of considerable strength before the whole art of war was changed by the invention of gunpowder. Its high battlemented walls of red granite, its lofty towers, postern gates, and inclined planes, vividly reminding the spectator of the illustrations in Froissart's chronicles, and the proud symbol of the Moghuls, the golden crescent, still gleaming on its pinnacles and cupolas, altogether present an imposing assemblage, which brings to the mind a thousand images of feudal glory. A few mail-clad knights, plumed and mounted, and riding down those precipitous descents which form a distinguishing characteristic of a fortress of the olden time, or some fair lady waving a scarf from a turreted height, alone are wanting, to transport the spectators back to the days of chivalry. Happily no attempt has been made to maintain the fort of Agra against a hostile force. The Moghuls surrendered it to the Jauts at once, and they in turn yielded it up almost without a blow to the army under Lord Lake; it has consequently escaped uninjured, and has been allowed to retain its primitive construction by a government which is under no apprehension from the surrounding native states. The walls of this fortress embrace an area of very considerable extent: an immense hall, formerly the place in which the Moghul emperors held their durbars, is now converted into an arsenal, and the Mootee Musjid, or pearl mosque, and the palace of Akbar, are both comprehended within the circuit of the fortifications. The palace, which is built entirely of white marble, is a very splendid fabric, and is still in excellent repair; the Jauts, the great destroyers of the works of their hated enemies, the Moghuls, having contented themselves with tearing down the silver ceilings. The principal hall is a superb apartment supported on pillars and arches in a noble style of architecture; there are a great many other suites of smaller chambers, highly decorated, the walls being inlaid with a mosaic work of flowers executed in an almost endless variety of cornelians, agates, blood-stone, lapis lazuli, and jasper: these beautiful apartments overlook the Jumna, commanding a lovely prospect of that blue and sparkling river, as it winds along banks planted with luxuriant gardens, every jutting point decked with some light and tasteful pavilion, and the towers and pinnacles of the splendid mausoleum of Etmun ud Dowlah, the father of Nourmahal, rising from amidst forest trees, rich in foliage and flowers: marble staircases lead to the flat roof of the palace, from which a much more extensive view is obtained; the whole forming a magnificent terrace, where, in the evening or at night, the inhabitants of the palace may enjoy a delightful promenade under skies balmy and bright almost beyond imagination, and in the midst of the most captivating scenery in the world; there are numerous small quadrangles and courtyards, intersecting this noble building, each has its parterre, its marble basins, or its fountains; multitudes of pigeons of various colours, blue, pink, brown, and green, nestle amid the pinnacles, adding the gleaming colours of their foliage to the flush of flowers, and the sparkling of the waters, flowing through channels scooped out of the pavement to

TAJ MAHAL,— AGRA.

receive them. This palace would form an appropriate residence for the new governor, could it be cooled to a temperature befitting European constitutions. During the rains, and in the cold season, it is often chosen for the abode of gentlemen employed in the public service, but it is not considered habitable in the hot winds, which would scarcely be excluded from its numerous doors and windows. The appearance of this imperial residence has been much improved during the late visit of the governor-general, who directed the removal of many extraneous buildings, erected with a view more to convenience than beauty, by occasional sojourners in the fort.

The palace of the great Akbar, though it may justly vie with the far-famed Alhambra, and is even superior to that celebrated building in the delicacy and finish of its ornaments, is eclipsed by the superior beauty of the pearl mosque, an edifice of which it is almost impossible to convey even the faintest idea, so exquisitely lovely is this scene of fairy splendour: were it formed of the pearl by which it is so aptly designated, its whiteness, purity, or brilliancy, could not be surpassed; it is difficult to suppose it the workmanship of human hands, and the rapt spectator cannot help fancying that some wondrous tale must be connected with a creation which appears to be of more than mortal origin. The dazzling resplendence of the material can only be compared to a flood of moonlight, but the admiration and astonishment which it calls forth is speedily absorbed by the higher species of delight excited by the chaste grandeur of the architecture; an immense quadrangle cloistered on three sides with a rich arcade, surmounted at intervals with octagonal pavilions, leads to a hall supported by several rows of arches, most beautifully springing out of each other, and crowned with a light dome; a marble basin is hollowed in the centre of the court, in the midst of which a fountain plays perpetually, adding its soothing murmurs to the calm and silvery radiance of the scene.

THE TAJ MAHAL, AT AGRA.

Whatsoever may be alleged against the character of Shah Jehan in his government of the vast empire which he partly won by his own sword, in his domestic relations, as a husband and a father, he is unimpeachable. The mausoleum, whose incomparable beauty excites the highest degree of wonder and admiration in all who approach it, is not only a record of his taste and magnificence, but of a virtuous, holy, and undying attachment, which has been equalled by few professing a purer creed, and has been surpassed by none. The conjugal affection of Shah Jehan for the Light of the World, as he delighted to call the lovely and pious sharer of his throne, lasted undiminished during a period of twenty years. Nor could death destroy the tie; when about to lose the object most beloved on earth, for ever, the emperor, it is said, while expressing his passionate regret, declared that he would erect a monument over her remains, excelling every other that the world could boast, in the same degree as she excelled all the daughters of the earth. If we estimate the beauty of Nour Jehan by that of her mausoleum, it must have been exquisite indeed.

The view taken of the Taj Mahal in the plate before us, is from the Jumna, which washes a wall of red granite, the boundary of the magnificent garden in which this splendid structure rises. The Taje itself stands upon a terrace or platform of white marble, the place of interment being in the centre immediately below the dome, and in this, the basement story. The steps leading to the platform occupy the front, together with the passage leading to the place of sepulture, which has no light save that afforded by the lamps which still burn above the tombs.

On the side towards the river, and the two others, are suites of apartments consisting of three rooms in each, the roofs, walls, and floors all of marble, and divided from each other by perforated marble screens ; so lavishly magnificent is even the foundation of this splendid palace. Upon the platform over these apartments, a perfect square, of one hundred and ninety yards, an octagonal building surmounted by a dome, rising amidst a beautiful cluster of open cupolas and minars, arrests the eye. It is entered by four gateways, two of which are seen in the plate, the whole being of white marble, even to the latticed frames of the windows, with the exception of a beautiful mosaic work of texts from the Koran, which surrounds the gateways : these inscriptions, inlaid in black marble, form a broad and elegant border. At each corner of the terrace there is a splendid minaret of white marble, a hundred and fifty feet in height.

Notwithstanding an air of formality imparted by these slight and beautiful columns, the group altogether is without a peer ; the contemplation of the chaste splendour of the material, and the exquisite felicity of the workmanship, affording never-tiring delight. The immense quantity of polished marble brought together, and the elegance of the forms in which it is disposed, give it a sort of superhuman grace ; we can scarcely believe it to be the work of men, or composed of less precious materials than mother of pearl. The exceeding richness of the ornaments, and the dazzling glitter of its snowy surface, suggest the idea of pearls, or moonbeams—something, in fact, which fairies might command, but far beyond the reach of mere mortal hands.

The doors of this superb building were formerly of silver, and the lofty crescent, gleaming from a spire thirty feet high, was, with the shaft that supported it, of solid gold. Both these tempting treasures were carried away by the Jauts, and materials of less value have been substituted by the present government.

To the right and left of the Taje, upon a lower platform or terrace, are two mosques of red granite, inlaid with white marble, and crowned with marble domes, both having very high claims to admiration, and completing a group of architectural beauty, which even the splendid Moghul has rarely, if ever, surpassed.

The interior of the Taje exceeds the promise given by its external magnificence : on a platform in the centre of a circular hall, are the sarcophaguses of Shah Jehan, and his beloved empress, enclosed within a carved screen of the most elaborate tracery and exquisite finish. These sarcophaguses, and the surrounding walls and screens, are covered with flowers and inscriptions of the most delicate mosaic work, in every variety of cornelian, agate, jasper, lapis lazuli, and other precious marbles. The flowers are the size of life, and so natural, that they appear as if freshly plucked and laid upon white satin: the shading is most beautifully true, five-and-thirty varieties of red cornelian occurring in a single leaf of a carnation.

The design of this building is attributed to the Emperor, but its execution was not wholly entrusted to native hands. Shah Jehan sent all over the world for skilful artists to execute his plans; and the beautiful embroideries of mosaic, for such they seem, were the works of men celebrated at Rome for their eminence in this branch of art. Round the hall containing the tombs of Shah Jehan and the peerless lady to whom this splendid shrine was raised, are several smaller apartments in the recesses formed by the octagonal shape of the building; marblestair-cases lead to the roof, whence the view over the Jumna, and across the gardens, is one of the loveliest imaginable.

Perhaps from no other point could persons who have never visited the Taje obtain so clear a notion of this singularly beautiful edifice, as from that chosen in the present drawing, where its pearly domes and towers are mirrored in the calm waters of the Jumna, but it requires a series of pictorial illustrations to convey an adequate idea of the exceeding splendour of a region of enchantment, which the brightest fancies of the poet or the painter have never surpassed.

On the side of the Taje opposite to the river, a large garden, too extensive for its formality to detract from its numerous beauties, luxuriant with standard peach, and other flowering trees, and celebrated for its vines and for its roses, tempers the glories of the dazzling structure beyond, by its embowering foliage and grateful shade. From the principal gateway, which forms the subject of another plate, and therefore needs no farther mention here, an avenue of cypress trees traverses the whole extent of this beautiful plantation.

It is utterly impossible for any language to convey a just idea of the impression made upon the mind by the appearance of the Taje, as it rises in virgin majesty at the end of a vista at once so beautiful, so solemn, and so appropriate. There is a melancholy sublimity about it, which touches and melts the heart; the eyes involuntarily gush out with tears; and many, who have scarcely heard the name of her who sleeps within that honoured pile, approach the mausoleum weeping. The effect is heightened by basins of white marble, fed by fountains, at equal distances, which occupy the whole line down the centre of the avenue, reflecting on their glassy surfaces the elegant though mournful cypress trees, in beautiful contrast with the pearly minarets and domes mingling in the splendid picture.

In wandering about this large and ever-blooming garden, rendered an Eden by its perpetual succession of flowers and fruits, the partial glimpses obtained through openings in the trees of the clustering buildings of the Taje, its graceful minarets, and the solid grandeur of the adjacent mosques, afford a higher degree of gratification to the spectators than the more comprehensive, and also more formal view, which is generally selected by the artist, when obliged to confine his work to one point. The Taje Mahal, which took eleven years to complete, is said to have been erected at the cost of seven hundred and fifty thousand pounds. The marble of which it is composed was conveyed by land from Kandahar, a distance of nearly six hundred miles; the granite employed in the walls of the garden, and the surrounding buildings, came from the Mewat hills in the neighbourhood. Shah Jehan intended to have built a similar structure on the opposite bank of the river, for the reception of his own remains, and to have connected both by a bridge of marble; but the troubles of his reign commenced before he could put this magnificent design into execution. His declining years were spent in confinement in the fort of Agra, and at his death his corpse was interred by the side of that which he had so highly honoured.

Arjemund Banu, the favourite wife of Shah Jehan, was the niece of the still more celebrated Nourmahal, who, after the murder of her first husband, Shere Afkun, was raised to the imperial throne by Jehanguire. The names by which this illustrious lady is distinguished (Nour Jehan, light of the world, Muntazi Zemani, the most exalted of the age, Moom Taza Mhal, and others) were conferred upon her in consequence of the high degree of estimation in which she was held throughout the empire. Her virtues and talents were assuredly of no mean order, and have been commemorated by testimony still more conclusive than the splendid trophy of her husband's affection. On the right bank of the Jumna from Agra to Delhi, there is a well at the distance of every ten or fifteen miles, made at the expense of this charitable princess, who, compassionating the sufferings of poor travellers from the dearth of water, directed that provision should be made for their comfort by a supply, which, on a journey between the two cities, she found would be very difficult of attainment by those who had not wealth at command. She was also famed for her piety, her hatred of idolatry being so great as to excite her indignation against the Portuguese, the rites and ceremonies of whose religion, savouring so much of pagan superstition, shocked her feelings, and rendered her their inveterate enemy. The British government has with laudable zeal taken the Taje Mahal under its especial protection; more than twelve thousand pounds have been expended on its repairs, the garden is kept in perfect order, and the whole is always open to European and native visitors. The latter take a great and natural pride in this superb memorial of former power. Upon a Sunday evening, when the fountains are playing, the garden exhibits gay groupes of shewy figures, variously attired, some with caftans of velvet, or brocade, bordered with gold; others, more gaudy, shining out in tinsel finery; and a plainer description clad in white garments, bound round with flowing shawls; while the very poorest classes crowd from the neighbouring city to this favourite spot, and whenever the doors of the interior are opened to an European, the native guardians not choosing to unlock them for every body, respectfully ask to be admitted in his train; a permission which is never refused.

MACAO.

The most untiring perseverance, the most exemplary patience, together with the practice of every diplomatic art which experienced politicians could devise, have not, during the course of many years, prevailed against the unabating caution of the Chinese government. British adventurers must still be content to share with the Portuguese the narrow settlement in which European traders are cooped up for the greater part of the year by their jealous neighbours. The occupation of Macao by a grant from the head of

MACAO.—CHINA.

the celestial empire to the Portuguese, as a reward for their services against the pirates infesting the islands at the mouth of the Canton river, took place on or about the year 1586.

Macao is completely insulated from the Chinese territories by a wall, which has been built across the isthmus for the purpose of preventing any communication with the interior: this boundary is strictly guarded, and the intercourse between Canton and the only refuge which Europeans are permitted to call their own, is carried on entirely by water. The settlement of Macao lies in latitude 22° 13′ N. and in longitude 113° 32′ E. about fifty miles from the mouth of the river: it is a picturesque-looking place, the shore being lined with the houses of the European residents, and the heights occupied by churches, convents, and forts, adding architectural beauty to the barren rocks on which they are erected. The bay possesses very considerable claims to admiration, and, though not particularly safe or commodious, especially at certain periods of the year, is finely enclosed by the abrupt peaks of the mountainous islands of Lantow and Lintin. The extraordinary clearness of the atmosphere in fine weather, the gay colours and singular forms of the boats, and the foreign air of the houses, offer a very interesting picture to a stranger; but the monotony becomes very tiresome to those condemned to make a long sojourn in this remote and isolated place.

The view in the accompanying engraving is taken from nearly the centre of the bay. The large buildings to the right are those belonging to the East India Company, and that distinguished by a pole, or flag-staff, is the Chinese chop or custom house. Though Macao nominally belongs to the Portuguese, the English have established their supremacy in the settlement, and very little cordiality subsists between the families of the two nations; their habits and manners do not assimilate, and their intercourse with each other is confined to mere visits of ceremony. Though picturesque and imposing in its external appearance, the town of Macao is dirty and irregular. There are no roads, and therefore no carriages; pedestrian exercise is performed over rough tracts of loose stones and rocks, and those who are unequal to the fatigue, and unwilling to peril their necks in the scramble, are conveyed about the town and its vicinity in clumsy chairs, the only equipage which is to be obtained.

The society is extremely limited, and forms no exception to the general characteristics of a confined circle; a superabundant quantity of tittle-tattle, and a vast deal of amusing and innocent scandal, supply the place of higher and more intellectual topics. The principal talk of the gentlemen is of opium, excepting upon occasions of great excitement, when the whole settlement is put into a ferment by some alarming feud between the Hong merchants and the supercargoes, or when some humiliating concession, long abandoned, and apparently set at rest, is again insisted upon by a government always desirous to recur to their ancient systems. The highest degree of hospitality is exercised in the most indiscriminating manner by the British residents of Macao. The stranger is welcome to every house, and there is a cover at every table whenever he chooses to take advantage of it; the interruption to the dull domestic routine afforded by casual visitors, can scarcely fail to be acceptable; and though there may be many who have weighed out tea, and speculated in opium until they can think and talk of nothing else, and therefore feel little interested in communications upon less important subjects, there are a few who wish to enlarge their knowledge of what is going on in other parts of the world, and even under the chilling influence of exile retain a lively curiosity concerning the novelties in polite literature and the arts, of which some faint rumour may have reached this sequestered settlement.

Macao is sometimes enlivened by the speculations of musical professors, and an Italian opera was at one time established there: whether the project proved sufficiently successful to induce these sons of Apollo to remain, we have as yet had no opportunity of learning. During a great part of the year, the settlement, dull at all times, is rendered still more so by the absence of the heads of families, who take their departure to Canton, whither their wives and daughters are not permitted to accompany them. An attempt to resist the strict regulations of the Chinese in this respect very nearly occasioned a serious breach between the two governments. An edict, issued in consequence of some remonstrances upon the subject, contains the following paragraph—the essence of the Chinese notions upon commercial speculations:—

"Since the said foreigners come to trade, it is only incumbent on them to obey implicitly the orders of government. If they dislike the restrictions as difficult to be endured, it is perfectly competent to them not to take the trouble to come so great a distance."

Such reasoning is unanswerable, and it is very clear that the right of conquest alone will enable Europeans to dictate the terms in which trade shall be carried on with the celestial empire.

DOWLATABAD.

This extraordinary fortress, which is situated upon the road between Ellora and Aurungabad, at the distance of seven miles from the latter place, was originally the work of the Hindoos, to whom it belonged, until 1294. These hill-fortresses were considered of great importance, while the Asiatic mode of warfare prevailed, and nature and art have combined to render Dowlatabad one of the strongest as well as the most remarkable of all the places of the kind in Hindoostan. A rocky hill, which in shape has been likened to a compressed bee-hive, rises abruptly from the plain at about a mile distant from the foot of the range so famed for its excavations, and of which it is supposed it must have been forcibly separated by some convulsion of the earth. The form and site of this eminence were particularly favourable for the exercise of the skill and patience of which Hindoo architects have left so many imperishable monuments. The height of this hill is about five or six hundred feet, and it is not more than a mile in circumference. The rock has been rendered precipitous by the labours of man, and forms round the foot of the hill a steep smooth wall, or scarp, of one hundred and fifty feet in height; a wide and deep ditch affords additional security to this inaccessible defence. Upon crossing the ditch, the ascent is through an excavation in the heart of the rock, which is carried in a most singular manner to the upper works, winding through the inmost recesses of the hill

THE FORTRESS OF DOWLUTABAD.

The commencement of this subterranean passage is exceedingly low, and can only be traversed in a stooping posture: but after a few paces, it leads into a lofty vault, which is illuminated by torches. From this hall, a gallery twelve feet high, and twelve feet broad, and not so steep as to be very fatiguing, until it approaches the summit, conducts the wondering visitor to the various halting places, where there are small trap-doors, whence narrow flights of steps lead to the ditch below. The design of these traps has given rise to a good deal of speculation, some persons supposing that they were intended as additional defences in the event of the passage being forced, while to others they appear totally unfitted for such a purpose. There is no light in this subterraneous passage, except that which is obtained from torches. The main avenue, for there are others branching out into store-houses cut in recesses in the rock, at a certain elevation opens into a cavity, about twenty feet square; this is defended by a large iron plate, which can be laid over the outlet in case of assault. The plate is furnished with a poker of gigantic dimensions, and should a besieging foe penetrate so far, the plate would be shut down, and a large fire kindled upon it: a hole five feet in diameter has been constructed, to convey a strong current of air to this furnace. Upon emerging from the earth, the road becomes steep and narrow, the hill is in many places covered with brushwood, and buildings are scattered over it. The house of the governor is large and handsome, and from the flagstaff the view is beautiful and extensive: the towns of Karguswarra and Rozah being plainly discernible over the range of hills in the neighbourhood. On this peak a large brass four-and-twenty pounder has been placed: the difficulty of the undertaking is said to have been immense, and only to be overcome by the persevering assiduity of an engineer, who, on the promise of being allowed to return to his own home, suffered no obstacle to relax his efforts, and after numerous trials accomplished his object at last. Dowlatabad is almost wholly destitute of ordnance, and under the present system of military operations has lost much of its importance: it does not command any road, pass, or country, and is now only interesting, as affording a very remarkable specimen of a hill fortress.

The Moghuls obtained possession of Dowlatabad at a very early period, and it was made an imperial city by Mahomed Tugleck, who gave it its present name; its former appellation, under the Hindoo Rajahs, being Deoghur. The emperor also attempted to transfer the seat of government from Delhi to the scene of his new conquest, but without success. When the Moghuls were driven out of the Deccan by the princes of the Carnatic, the latter obtained possession. It was at one time in the hands of the French, who, however, did not keep it long, their troops being withdrawn into the Carnatic by the command of M. Lally. The Mahrattas afterwards made themselves masters of it, but in 1776 it was added to the nizam of Hyderabad, and has continued under his descendants ever since. The protection and friendship accorded by the British government to this power, has enabled it to maintain possession of the fortress, and the reigning prince has rendered good service in return, by co-operating with his allies when his assistance was required, or maintaining a strict neutrality when not wanted in the field. But though secure upon his throne, and at peace with his neighbours, the suspicion inseparable from

Asiatic modes of government, renders the post of honour conferred upon the officer entrusted with the command of Dowlatabad, one of discomfort and danger. The family of the governor of this jealously-guarded fortress are detained as hostages at Hyderabad. Under the Moghul Emperor Akbar, and Jehanguire, no one was permitted to retain so important a command for more than three years; and though great changes have been effected since those days of tyranny and despotism, the country still suffers under the desolating influence of Moslem rule: it is thinly peopled, and though the extensive and fertile plains possess rich soils, and are intersected with many streams, they have the appearance of a desert.

EXCAVATED TEMPLE OF KYLAS—CAVES OF ELLORA.

Amongst the numerous astonishing works of art left to excite the surprise and admiration of posterity, the Temple of Kylas, which has been justly termed the paradise of the gods, must be considered the most extraordinary, even in a land of wonders. It forms one of the numerous excavations of the far-famed Ellora. This mountain range, beautiful in itself, watered by a fine stream, which descends in broad cascades from ledge to ledge of the rugged eminences, is wrought into temples and palaces, partly subterranean, and partly isolated, formed of the living rock, and decked with a redundance of ornament, which utterly defies description. Kylas is the finest and most perfect of the excavated temples of Ellora; the approach to it is more beautiful, and it is more highly-finished, than those in its neighbourhood. The central building, of which a representation is given in the Plate, rises in the midst of a wide area, all scooped and cut from the solid rock. From the hill-side it exhibits a very fine front. A splendid gateway is flanked on either side by towering battlemented heights, covered with sculpture, and containing many apartments. Over the portal, which is exceedingly lofty, there is a balcony, which is supposed to be intended for a music gallery, (Nöbat Khana.) The passage through this gateway is richly adorned with sculpture, in which the eight-armed goddess Bhawani appears: it leads into a vast area, cut down through the hill, as represented in the annexed engraving, and in the centre of which stands the Temple, a structure raising mingled emotions of amazement, pleasure, and reverential awe. Every part of it is richly and elaborately carved with a profusion of ornament, and a minuteness of finish, of which it would be vain to attempt to convey the most distant idea. Every portion of the exterior and interior, which comprises several stories, and the roof likewise, is carved into columns, pilasters, friezes, and pediments, embellished with the representations of men and animals, singly or in groups, and accompanied with all the attributes which have rendered the Hindoo pantheon the most populous assemblage of the kind. The temple, which is excavated from the upper regions of the rock, and, as we have before stated, stands alone, is connected with the gateway by a bridge or platform, also cut out of the solid rock; the surrounding galleries or colonnades are separated from the main building by a distance of one hundred and fifty feet. The central fane rears its proud crest to the height of a hundred feet, being one immense block of isolated excavation, upwards of five hundred feet in

EXCAVATED TEMPLE OF KYLAS,-CAVES OF ELLORA.

SKELETON GROUP IN THE RAMESWUR, CAVES OF ELLORA.

circumference, containing many splendid apartments, and furnished with windows, doorways, and staircases. Beyond, and forming the boundary of the court which surrounds it, are three magnificent galleries supported upon pillars, and containing stories of the Hindoo mythology, represented in compartments of the stone scarping, in which forty-two gigantic figures of gods and goddesses appear. This superb piazza is eleven feet broad, and in some places fourteen in height, but the elevation varies, and it is not quite complete. Part of the south side of the area is occupied by chambers, all richly and lavishly embellished, one of which contains groups of female figures, so exquisitely sculptured, that even Grecian art has scarcely surpassed the beauty of the workmanship. In the court are the remnants of colossal elephants; there is also an obelisk, nearly entire; and the splendid square temple of the bull Nundi, forming a part of the pagoda, which fills up the central space, may be seen from the spot in which the drawing was taken. Pen and pencil, however accurate and vivid, can afford very ineffectual aid in a task so utterly beyond their powers. The excess and variety of the objects which present themselves to the bewildered gazer's eye, as he enters upon this enchanted ground, actually become painful, until the tumultuous sensations they arouse in the mind subside, and calm contemplation succeeds astonishment, awe, and delighted wonder. The popular belief amongst the natives, that these singularly beautiful works owe their origin to preternatural power, appears to be too justly founded to be contested; for, with all the light of knowledge possessed by people of the highest intellectual attainments, it is difficult to take a more sober view of a scene, which seems so far to surpass the feeble powers of man. Conjecture is completely baffled in its endeavours to trace these mighty works to their founders. Though still frequented by a few fakeers, they are not held in any reverential esteem by the Hindoo population. Their sacred character has been utterly lost in the lapse of ages, and it can only be said that those by whom such gigantic undertakings were projected, must have been a highly intellectual and imaginative people, possessed of vast resources, and living in times of perfect security and peace. The rock from which the temples of Ellora are wrought, is hard red granite, and, from every peak and pinnacle of the excavated mountain, the eye roams over scenes of romantic beauty.

SKELETON GROUP IN THE RAMESWAR—CAVES OF ELLORA.

The researches of the most profound and diligent antiquaries have failed to establish the claims of Râm and Seeta to the honour of the sculptures representing the nuptials of some of the favourite Hindoo deities, which embellish the temple of Rameswar. Sew and Parwuttee, according to the opinion of a very erudite writer, have a better right to be considered as the actors in the scene; but, though there may be a difference of opinion respecting the identity of the parties, all agree in admitting that the various groups which fill the compartments of this highly-finished excavation, surpass in interest, and are not inferior in beauty, to any which appear in the larger and more important temples.

Rameswar, when measured with the gigantic works in its neighbourhood, is of comparatively small dimensions. It consists of a fine hall, seventy-two feet long, and about fifteen in height; there is another temple, thirty-one feet square, in a recess of the Rameswar; the principal apartment is supported by pillars and pilasters, of admirable proportions, and the walls and roof are covered with figures, chiefly representing the frolics and sports of deities, relaxing from the cares of state, and indulging themselves, like mere mortals, in dance and revelry. The group represented in the plate, which has been the subject of much curiosity and discussion, forms a striking contrast to the joyousness which distinguishes the other compartments: the principal figures are skeletons, and the attendant Brahmins, who are apt to substitute popular tales for the less amusing theories of learned men, give their own version of the story to all the visitors. They say that the skeletons commemorate the guilt and punishment of a wicked family who plundered the temples, and, having enriched themselves with the pillage of the gods, and the hardly-gathered earnings wrung from the people, hoarded this ill-gotten wealth, thus provoking the vengeance of Heaven, which descended upon them in the manner described in the sculpture; while in a famishing state, from long deprivation and abstinence, they had the additional horror of seeing their riches carried away from them before their eyes, the supposed plunderer being the figure in the corner flying off with a bag. This story is scouted by all the antiquaries, and the Brahmins, though they persist in the relation, are not exceedingly tenacious of its authority, but, while acknowledging that they may be in error, agree that the skeletons represented are rakshesas (demons.) It is supposed that this singular group partly consists of victims intended to be sacrificed at a festival in which the Now Ratree, seven females sculptured in an adjoining compartment, are engaged, and that the central figure, the father of a starving family, is selling his wife and children for the purpose. There is so little interest, excepting to the few scholars anxious to throw light upon the monstrous superstitions of the Hindoos, in any thing relating to their cumbrous mythology, that the visitors of Ellora are generally more content to admire the skill of the sculpture, than to attempt to convince themselves of the precise nature of the subject; a very justifiable indifference, where there is so little to be gained by inquiry and research.

The solemn loneliness of these caves, their wild seclusion on the mountain's brow, remote from the populous assemblies of man, and the beauty and grandeur which strike the eye on every side, and fill the mind with wonder, must satisfy the pilgrims to Ellora. If we turn from the numberless subjects of doubt and difficulty which the most accomplished Oriental scholars have laboured vainly to elucidate, to the human hands which have wrought the miracles we see around, the attempt is equally hopeless; their history is not less obscure than that of the skeleton group which has perplexed so many of the wise, and the curiosity which they excite is far more lively and intense.

The absence of that religious veneration which the Hindoos are so prone to shew to the objects of their idolatry, remains unaccounted for; no one can presume to guess by whom these mighty excavations were formed, or why they have been abandoned by the multitudes still paying bigoted adoration to the deities whose effigies are disregarded in the most splendid of their shrines.

THUBARE,

There is no clue to guide us through the labyrinths of thought raised by these sublime reliques of a former age; we are compelled to remain in perfect ignorance, and feel that all our speculations must be idle and unprofitable. A few poor Brahmins still haunt the scene, but they admit that it has lost its sanctity, and the scanty profit which they derive from visitors who come to gaze on the wonders of the mountain, is drawn from the purses of Christian pilgrims, anxious to satiate their eyes with splendours far surpassing the imaginary creations of the genii, as decribed in Oriental fiction. To them are the salutations Ram! Ram! and Mahadeo! raised by the children of the soil, grateful for the bounty which has been scattered amongst them, and proud that the objects of their own worship, and the magnificent works of their predecessors, should attract the attention of their foreign rulers. The visits of Anglo-Indians to the temples of Ellora are, however, not so general or so frequent as might be inferred from the intellectual requirement of that class of the society. A vast proportion of Europeans resident during many years in the Bombay presidency, know little, except by hearsay, of the extraordinary excavations in their neighbourhood; comparatively few make a journey purposely to see them, and it is to the indolence and apathy manifested by the greater portion of our Eastern adventurers, that so small a number of the tourists and travellers, who have ransacked every other portion of the globe, have bent their steps to British India.

THUBARE—RED SEA.

The parched and sandy desert, the withering blast of the hot simoom sweeping over the howling wilderness, the utter desolation and horror which invest the burning wastes which spread themselves along the shores of the Red Sea, possess a peculiar and powerful interest over the mind. None who have ever delighted in the perusal of Oriental travels, or who have luxuriated in Oriental fictions, have failed to wander in idea along these arid tracts; where the widely spread caravan plods its weary way through seas of sand, or rests beneath the tall date-trees which shade some long-desired well; where troops of wild Bedouins scour across the plain, scattering death in their path; and where at last the minarets and cupolas of the holy city of Mecca arise to cheer the fainting spirit; or the delicious gardens and fountains of Damascus reward the traveller for all the perils he has passed.

Thubare is a small haven on the Red sea, in which Arab vessels trading up or down the gulf find a secure place of anchorage for the night. This cove is rendered peculiarly desirable, from the abundance of pure and perfectly fresh water, which may be procured from wells dug close to the shore at the head of the bay. It likewise affords an interesting specimen of the mountain scenery of Arabia, the bare and barren peaks which lift their summits to the torrid sky, the deep and desolate ravines, scantily clothed at intervals with rushes, coarse grass, and stunted bushes, while imagination may picture the dreary expanse beyond, crusted with salt, or torn up in billows by the rushing blast. Few living creatures give animation to these unfruitful wilds; a few jerboas, hares, and guanas, may occasionally be seen, or a herd of antelopes where the pasturage is more abundant. The birds are equally scarce; half a dozen desert partridges, and the same number of blue pigeons, are only to be met with during a long march over a flat exposed country, where the range of the eye is only bounded by the horizon. The Bedouins, less scrupulous than the more orthodox followers of the prophet, do not hesitate to eat jerboas, guanas, and even lizards and snails, provided that they are killed according to the prescribed method: they believe that all wild animals, with the exception of the hog, were created for the use of man; and the scantiness of provision in the desert certainly affords a good excuse for some abatement of the prejudices of their religion.

The present state of the soil of "Araby the blest" is not very favourable to cultivation: in the immediate neighbourhood of the towns and villages, various kinds of grain and a few vegetables are raised, but the fruits are scarce and bad; the apricots spungy, the figs hard, and the water-melons dry, the date trees, which are nourished with a constant supply of water, afford the most abundant crop, and may be esteemed the staple commodity of the land. In the bazaars, camel's flesh of an inferior quality is exposed for sale. The Arabian camel offers the finest specimen of his class; it is slighter in its form, and more active, than that of Egypt, which is a large heavy animal, incapable of moving at a swift pace, and requiring a large portion of corn and forage for its support. The Arabian camel can subsist on the bushes which are to be found on all the sand-hills of the desert; if lightly laden, it will get over the ground in a very rapid manner, and it is also found efficient as a beast of draught as well as of burden. The guns of Ibrahim Pacha were principally drawn by camels from the Red Sea to Deriah. This "ship of the desert," as it has been aptly styled by Arab writers, could alone enable wayfarers to traverse the vast extents of sand which separate the habitable places from each other. Large caravans are usually divided into parties composed of from ten to fifty camels, each person keeping his own domestics and baggage around him. An advanced guard, to which the guides are attached during the night march, points out the way by means of a lanthorn elevated on a pole, and affixed to the saddle of the leading camel. This beacon, like the top light of a commodore's ship, directs the movements of the convoy; and, to keep the caravan from spreading itself too widely, pistols are discharged at intervals from front to rear. Notwithstanding the distress and danger which beset the path, the horrors of thirst and famine, the aggravations of every difficulty from the carelessness of the Arabs, who disregard all the precautions requisite to lessen the discomforts of the journey, halting inconsiderately at inconvenient places, and wasting the supplies of water conveyed in skins, when wells are not to be found, and the continual alarms occasioned by predatory tribes of Bedouins, the exceeding sanctity of the cities of Mecca and Medina invite pilgrims from every part of the East.

The establishment of a new sect of Mohammedans, more intolerant and fanatic than any of their predecessors, rendered for a series of years the performance of the duty enjoined to all true believers still more formidable. It is only lately that Ibrahim Pacha has succeeded in destroying the power of the Wahabees; he marched a large force across the desert to Deriah, the seat of their dominion, attacked the place, and, after a most obstinate resistance took it, together with the Wahabee chief, his family, and all their treasure, which was immense, including the spoils of Mecca, which they plundered when the holy city fell under their subjugation. Abdoolla ben Saood, the chief, and his children, were sent to Constantinople, and put to death there, a measure which exterminated the sect: a son of Abdoola's, by an Abyssinian slave, was still in the desert in 1830, but he has no followers of wealth or consequence. The Wahabees were particularly dangerous to pilgrims from Hindoostan, who usually made their journey from Calcutta to Bombay by water, and were consequently in constant peril of being taken by the pirates which infested this navigation. The Wahabee tenets are opposed to those of the two grand divisions of the Mohammedan religion, the Sheeas, and the Soonnees. The Sheeas maintain the prophet's son-in-law Ali to be equal to the prophet himself, which the Soonnees deny. These latter, considering the Sonna, or book of traditions, as a work of authority, charge the Sheeas with discrediting it, as well as with corrupting the true faith with new ceremonies and usages. The devotions of the Sheeas are paid principally at the tombs of the Imams of Kurbalahee Moullah; that of their father Ali, at Nugf Ushruf; and that of the Soonnees at the house of God at Mecca, and at Medina.

The religion of the Wahabees, if that can be called a religion which seems only to have been instituted as a cloak for indiscriminate plunder, differs wholly from these two; they assert that the Koran itself has been corrupted, and the real faith changed by the present Mussulmans, and a syllable of difference in any one from the Wahabee faith, forms a sufficient warrant for his instant death. A very interesting account of the capture of a Hindoostanee gentleman of rank, Nawab Abbas Khooly Khan, has been lately translated from the Persian of his personal narrative; an extract from this curious and authentic document,* which is not in general circulation, will shew the respect paid to the British power on the shores of the Red Sea; for the prisoner owed his life to his being a subject of the king of England; and also the opinion which the unsubdued followers of the prophet entertain of those who submit to Christian dominion.

"Ameer Hassan," says the Newab, "then asked me my religion, to which I replied that it was to him of little importance whether I was a Sheea or a Soonnee, as the Wahabees indiscriminately killed and plundered both the one and the other. Quitting this topic of conversation, he asked me why I had come from Hindostan? I answered, that I had been despatched on business from the Lord Governor General Saheb, to the king of Iran, Futteh Ally Shah, at Tehran. He observed, "You call yourself a Mussulman, and yet serve the Christians." "What," said I, "is that to me? am I singular in this respect? Thousands, nay, lacks of individuals, serve the English; and can I, who reside in their country, do otherwise? I, my family, and relations, live under their protection, and from them have, in all times of tyranny, oppression, or calamity, found refuge, and passed my time in security." He said, "Feringhees are infidels; he who serves, and praises, or esteems them, is himself an infidel, and deserves death." I replied, "Whoever eats another person's salt, and would not be faithful to that person, is a base-born irreligious

* To Robert Neave, Esq., of the Bengal Civil Service, the translator, the writer is indebted for the extract which is subjoined.

man, and from men of noble birth and exalted station look not for ingratitude." Ameer Abdoolla, and the Cazee, who were sitting near Ameer Hassan, observed, "The people of Hindoostan, and that part of the country, are undoubtedly all Kafirs, and Mooshriks, and liable to be put to death, if they be not converted and become as one of us." "Gracious powers!" I exclaimed, "the holy prophet of God himself could not in his time bring the whole world to believe his religion, nor make all mankind Mussulmans; is it likely that Abdool Asseez, or Saood, should render their self-invented religion current in the whole of Arabia?" In another part of the conversation, the Ameer said, "You have several times made use of the word Saheb, as Lord Saheb, and Bruce Saheb, (Resident of Bushire) and for this reason alone you deserve punishment; what is the meaning of terming a Kafir Saheb? the word Saheb belongs to God alone." The Nawab replied, "You have said that God alone is Saheb, or master, and you ask why I call a Feringhy Saheb? I answer, God is in truth the master of every thing, and higher than all other masters; as yet, however, no one has ever termed him Alla Saheb, or Khode Saheb, besides, those I speak of the Lord of all things has exalted, lacks of people call them Saheb, and pay them reverence and respect: it is not myself only, but thousands of others, and if you say it is improper, of what importance will your prohibition be, or who will heed it?"

THE WATER PALACE, MANDOO.

The tumults and wars which during a long period distracted the Rajpoot states, have left the still beautiful and once flourishing city of Mandoo in desolation and ruin. It stands on the flat tabular platform of a mountain belonging to the Vindyhan range, but which is separated from the neighbouring hills by a wide chasm—one of those gigantic works, which, though a freak of nature, bears a close resemblance to the designs of man. The appearance is that of an artificial ditch, of enormous dimensions. Over this, to the north, is a broad causeway, which at some seasons forms the only approach, the surrounding ravine being filled with water during the rains. This passage is guarded by three gateways, still entire, placed at a considerable distance from each other; the last being on the summit of the hill, which is ascended by a winding road cut through the rock. The masses of ruined buildings which spring amidst a redundance of vegetation, apparently the unchecked growth of ages, somewhat resemble those of the city of Gour in Bengal, where the forest has intruded upon the courts and halls of palaces; but the buildings at Mandoo are upon a more splendid scale, and they occupy a better situation upon an elevated height; both are almost equally left to the exclusive dominion of wild and savage beasts. A few Hindoo fakeers compose the whole of the human population resident in the city boasting so many remains of architectural beauty.

In former times, Mandoo was the capital of the Dhar Rajahs. It afterwards fell into the hands of the Patan conquerors of Malwa, and subsequently submitted to the great Acbar, who appeared before the walls in person. The prevailing style of the architecture is Afghan, and some of the specimens are the finest which that splendid race have left in India; the material is chiefly a fine calcarious red stone, but the

THE WATER PALACE.—MANDOO.

COOTUB MINAR, DELHI.

mausoleum of Hossein Shah, one of the most remarkable relics still existing, is composed entirely of white marble, brought from the banks of the Nerbudda. The Tehaz Ka Mahal, ship, or, as we have rendered it, water palace, is erected upon an isthmus which divides two large tanks of water from each other; the situation is exceedingly picturesque, and the calm, quiet beauty of the building, particularly when reflected from the glassy surface of the mirror which stretches itself below on either side, affords an object of delightful though pensive contemplation to the traveller who has come suddenly upon this wreck of former splendour.

The decay of Mandoo took place more than a century before Malwa became tributary to the British government. For a long period it formed an occasional retreat for the Bheels, predatory tribes, who having ravaged the surrounding country, established themselves at different times in the strong fortresses of the city: these marauders, overawed by the military force at Mhow and other places, no longer dare encroach upon the territories of their neighbours, and, with the exception of the few devotees before mentioned, desolate creatures, the jackall, the vulture, the serpent, and the wolf, retain undisputed possession of the halls and gardens, so mournfully attesting the former magnificence of a city overspread with jungle, and abandoned to the beasts of the field. Mandoo is occasionally visited by parties of officers quartered at Mhow, who derive a melancholy gratification in wandering over the scene of fallen greatness; for the most exuberant and buoyant spirit becomes depressed by the solemn stillness and utter desolation of this unbroken solitude. The famous grass oil, so much in esteem all over India, is obtained in great abundance from the herbage which covers the face of the country round Mandoo, and which loads the air with perfume. Its medicinal qualities are said to be very powerful, especially in all rheumatic complaints, sprains, &c.; and in consequence of its reputation, it is frequently adulterated at Calcutta, where it sells at a high price.

COOTUB MINAR.—DELHI.

The beauty and grandeur of the splendid column which rises in towering majesty amid the ruins of Old Delhi, has been universally acknowledged: it is supposed to be the highest in the world. The base, which is circular, forms a polygon of twenty-seven sides, and the exterior is fluted to the third story into twenty-seven circular and angular divisions, the flutings varying in each compartment. There are four balconies running round the pillar, the first at ninety feet from the ground, the second at one hundred and forty, the third at one hundred and eighty, and the fourth at two hundred and three feet: the summit was crowned with a majestic cupola of red granite, but this, at the time in which the present view was taken, had fallen in, and does not appear in the plate. The entire height of the Minar is two hundred and forty-two feet. The stone of which this magnificent pillar is composed, is principally red granite, but there is an admixture of black and white marble, the upper division being entirely formed of the latter material. An irregular spiral staircase, in which there are many openings for the admission of light and air, leads to the top; but this ascent, only a short time ago, was difficult and even perilous, in consequence of the dilapidated state of the building. The British government, however, with a praiseworthy desire to rescue so valuable a relic of antiquity from impending ruin, caused the flight, which consists of about three hundred steps, to be restored. The undertaking was somewhat difficult: Major Smith of the Engineers, who was employed in superintending it, being obliged to remove several of the large stones near the foundation.

The remains of an unfinished mosque in the close vicinity of the Minar, and the absence of any authenticated account of these various buildings, have given rise to the numerous conjectures which puzzle the mind, while contemplating this mysterious wonder springing out of darkness and oblivion. To the eastward extends a court enclosed by a high wall, and surrounded on two sides by arcades formed of pillars, in the richest style of Hindoo architecture; the domes are particularly elegant, and were evidently formed before a knowledge of the principles of the arch had reached the country: arcades of the same description, but with little ornament, extend to the south and east of the Minar. Close under the tower, the remains of one of those superb portals common to the buildings of the Moghuls is seen in the engraving. This splendid entrance, and the accompanying line of arches, is supposed to be the east front of an intended mosque, which was commenced under the reign of Mohammed Ghori, by his viceroy, Cootub, but never completed; and though of equal antiquity with the Minar, there is no sufficient reason for the belief that it was to have been attached to it. The archway of this gate is sixty feet in height, and the ornaments with which it is embellished are matchless: they are cut with the delicacy of a seal engraving, and the edges remain to this day perfectly sharp, and uninjured by the elemental conflicts they have sustained during the lapse of many centuries: the arcade which stretches beneath is of granite, and covered with inscriptions highly and minutely finished, according to the usual style of the Patans, who are said to build like giants, and to embellish like jewellers. From the top of the Cootub Minar the view is sublime: the eye wanders for miles over a sea of ruins, in which the Mausoleums of Humaioon and Sufter Jung alone remain entire. The river Jumna rolls its silver currents through the midst, making large curves, as it glides, snake-like, along. In the back ground, the large feudal towers of Selimgurgh rear their dark turreted heights in gloomy grandeur; and, still farther in the distance, the white and glittering mosques of modern Delhi appear amidst the dark green foliage of the surrounding trees.

In visiting the Cootub Minar, its astonishing height, surprising strength, the beauty of its proportions, the richness of the materials, the elegance of its ornaments, and the dreary grandeur of the surrounding scene, so completely fill the mind with almost tumultuous sensations of pleasure, not wholly unmixed with awe, that nothing more seems wanting to increase the interest which it creates; but when less absorbed in the contemplation of its stately and solemn beauty, the absence of traditional tales connected with so wonderful a monument of past ages, is attended with a feeling of disappointment; a void is left in the heart, when baffled imagination relinquishes the vain attempt to dive into the secrets of the time-worn tower.

EL WUISH.—RED SEA.

EL WUISH,—RED SEA.

El Wuish forms another of those small havens upon the northern coast of the Red Sea, to which Arab vessels, in that difficult navigation, hasten to take shelter during the night, or on the approach of bad weather. It lies towards the upper part of this land-locked gulf of the Indian Ocean, and is distinguished from other coves upon the coast by its magnificent back-ground of lofty mountains, whose dazzling peaks glitter in the noon-day sun. The surveys lately made upon the Red Sea, with a view to the establishment of a constant communication by means of steam between Europe and India, must lead to great improvements in the construction and management of Arab vessels, which at present, though exceedingly picturesque, are clumsy and inconvenient; little, if any, advancement having been made in nautical science since the earliest period of naval architecture. The necessity of some change in the method of building and preparing Arab vessels for sea, has been very strongly exemplified in the narrative of the Nawab Abbas Kooly Khan, one of the few Asiatic travellers who have written an account of their voyages; a translation, from the Persian, of this interesting document, published in Bengal, but which has not yet appeared in England, affords a very curious and authentic description of the Arab buglohs, as they are manned and equipped at the present day. Through the spirited exertions of Ibrahim Pacha, the headless trunks of the victims of the Wahabee pirates are no longer washed on shore along these dreary coasts; but the ill-conditioned craft which tempt the dangers of those rocks and shoals, so inimical to the navigation of the Red Sea, are as little able as heretofore to surmount the difficulties of the passage.

The Nawab, after remaining four months in the expectation of the arrival of a British ship, to convey himself and his family to Bombay, was induced to embark on board an Arab trader, under the protection of the English flag. He gave a thousand rupees (one hundred pounds) for the passage of his party, and put to sea in an evil hour. "It is worthy of remark," observes the Nawab, "as the first proof of our ill fortune, that, before our embarkation, this unlucky vessel had of herself grounded, and beat a hole in her bottom, so that they were obliged, in order to mend her, to unload and reload; and though it had remained in port two months, the nakhoda (captain) had not got her properly mended, or watered: had this been the case, we might have sailed when we pleased, and no one known any thing of us; but, besides three hundred souls, there were nearly in the whole seventy horses on board, while, from his extreme folly, there was hardly more than two days' water, so that we were obliged to coast along, stopping at every island and harbour to get a fresh supply. The spies gave daily intelligence to the Wahabees, so that very shortly two buglas appeared ahead of us. As they were a considerable way off, the nakhoda and moullim (mate) began looking through their telescopes, but were at a loss to make out whether they were friends or foes. About mid-day, the vessels had approached nearer, on which the nakhoda began to make preparations for battle, by loading some of the guns, and placing boards; but they appeared so afraid, that one would have thought they had lost their senses. As the harbour of Bugoo was near, we cast anchor there for the night, since it is an ancient custom not to attack vessels in harbour: and if any such attempt is made, the people of the island afford the attacked every assistance, that they may escape the disgrace of the violation of their ports. On board the bugla there were plenty of fire-arms of every description; fourteen cannon, two hundred muskets, nearly four hundred spears, and powder and ball in abundance; but there was not an individual capable of using them, and scarce one, indeed, of common courage. The two buglas went out of sight after we had cast anchor; and the nakhoda, inferring from this that they were not enemies, resumed his spirits. 'Do not,' said I, 'forget these words of mine—they are hostile; but, seeing the night closing in, and us at anchor in harbour, have left us for the present, to lull us into a false security, and draw us out of our place of refuge; to-morrow they will again make their appearance, so do not quit the port until you have good reason to suppose us safe.' The nakhoda, (may his household be cursed!) turned a deaf ear, and sailed as usual. We had hardly proceeded half a coss ere the morning of our calamity appeared, and the sun of our approaching misfortune became manifest: no sooner had the day commenced, than, from that quarter to which we had seen the two buglas retire, five vessels made their appearance. The writer, the moullin, the vakeel, seacunnies, and sailors, but especially that cursed Abdool Kurreem himself, were stricken with fear, their blood curdled in their veins, and their faces became of a cadaverous hue. I turned to him, and said, 'Why, what is this? notwithstanding all the advice received, and the entreaties made, you would not listen, and now see you have destroyed us all.' His mouth was parched with fear, he with difficulty stuttered out, 'How could I tell?' 'What has happened,' I replied, 'is irremediable; for the future act wisely and firmly; if you continue in this state of indecision, your example will infect the crew, and what will then be the case? As yet the enemy's ships are distant, and an hour or more will elapse before they can come up with us. Give orders that this grass, which covers the deck and encumbers the guns, be removed; what is necessary for the horses, put down below, and cast the rest overboard. Clean the decks, load the guns, and place three or four careful men by each: distribute the muskets and spears to the people, and station them on various parts of the vessel.'

"Abdool Kurreem, standing like a pillar of stone, spoke nothing, and heeded not what was said to him; but Abdi Ahummud, the second in command, who was a boisterous blustering fellow, and courageous enough, if you might judge from his speech, cried out, 'This battle is sea fighting, and not land warfare; in this case we must at least know better than you, so do not interrupt us, just sit still in peace, and see the sport, how, with these cannon on deck, I will send such a shower of balls as will knock the enemy to pieces and sink them. If we should happen to get the worst of the battle, I can easily manage to set fire to the two hundred maunds of gunpowder in the hold, and blow us all up together.' 'What a wonderful contrivance!' said I; 'it is very probable, I think, that you will do this. I see how it is, the bugla is as good as gone.' The Nawab proved a true prophet: when the time for action arrived, the rudder broke away and became useless, all the powder and ball upon the deck had been hidden under the provender for the horses; that which was below had been locked up, and the key lost; the crew called to the

RUINS,-OLD DELHI.

carpenter to refit the helm, and to break open the powder magazine; and in the hurry and confusion the vessel was boarded, and the people cut to pieces by the Wahabees."

Abbas Kooly Khan was one of those numerous pilgrims to Mecca and Medina, whom no danger or hardship can deter from visiting the tombs of the Imaums, and braving the perils which beset them, whether they make the journey by land or by water. Since the period of his voyage, the Arab vessels have sustained no improvement, putting to sea in the most rickety condition imaginable; disregarding all quarantine laws, and, in unhealthy seasons, scattering plague and pestilence wheresoever they touch. Nor has the spread of civilization yet extended landways along these desolate shores. The recent murder of Mr. Taylor, one of the most indefatigable of the promoters of steam navigation, affords a melancholy proof that the Bedouin character remains the same; but much may be hoped from the increasing intercourse with Europeans, which will be the result of Hugh Lindsey's voyages on the Red Sea. Travellers amongst the last arrivals, who have journeyed overland from Bombay, report that Ibrahim Pacha has determined upon making a rail-road across the isthmus: the echoes which have lately been startled by the paddles of a steam-engine, may soon learn to repeat sounds equally new and strange; and there is abundant reason to believe that a change, not more striking than sudden, is about to take place throughout the whole of those countries of the East, which for so long a period have remained in ignorance and barbarism.

RUINS,—OLD DELHI.

Amidst misshapen fragments, prostrate masses of stone, where the mosque of the faithful and the pagoda of the idolater lie indiscriminately together in one wide sea of ruin; the circular towers, which appear in the plate, still retain a considerable portion of their pristine beauty, and afford a pleasing relief to the eye, weary of the utter desolation and horror extending over so large a surface along the site of Old Delhi. It is not known, at the present day, to whose memory the monument, occupying the centre of the quadrangle flanked by these towers, was raised, but the existing portion shews that formerly it must have been a splendid embellishment of this once magnificent scene. The tomb is erected upon a terrace or platform, supported by arches, with a round tower surmounted by an open cupola at each angle, that which occupies the foreground of the engraving being the only one remaining in a tolerable state of preservation. This beautiful relic of other days is found at the northern extremity of the ruins of the former city, and about a mile from the walls of modern Delhi. In the period of its splendour, this ancient capital of the Patan and Moghul emperors was said to cover a space of twenty square miles, and the ruins are strewed over a plain nearly equal in extent. Before the Mahommedan invasion, it had been a place of great renown, many of the remains of Hindoo architecture dividing the interest with those of the Moslem conquerors: the sepulchres of one hundred and eighty thousand saints and martyrs, belonging to the faithful, were, it is said, to be found amidst the wrecks of temples and palaces, before all had crumbled into the undistinguishable mass which now renders the greater part of the scene so desolate. In the time of its glory, groves and gardens spread their luxuriant garlands over a soil now so parched, that not a bamboo could be found at the time that the staircase of the Cootub Minar was in too ruinous a state to admit of its ascent, to form a scaffolding to reach its summit on the outside.

The commencement of the last stage of the decline of Old Delhi must be dated from the period in which Shah Jehan founded the modern city; but, for a long time subsequently to the transfer of its inhabitants to its more flourishing neighbour, it retained a portion of its former beauty. In the days of Shah Jehan, the road through Agra to Lahore was shaded on either side by a fine avenue of mango trees, and, at the distance of every three miles, a well and a minar offered refreshment and repose to the traveller. The towers and the trees have totally disappeared, and the greater number, if not the whole of the wells, have been choked up and abandoned, so great has been the havoc and destruction occasioned by the numerous wars, which have ravaged this ill-fated portion of Hindoostan. The last decisive battle fought between the Moslem and the Hindoo, and which secured to the former the supremacy over Indraput, occurred six hundred years ago. The work of devastation has continued, with little intermission, ever since; the glories of the Patan and Moghul monarchies being often obscured by invasions and rebellions, while the long series of reverses and disasters following the reign of Aurungzebe completed the catalogue of misfortunes which reduced Delhi to its present miserable condition. The wrongs of the ancient possessors of the land have been avenged in Moslem blood by the friends and the foes of the prophet. To the devastations of Nadir Shah Kuzzilbashes, the work of modern times, those of the Jauts succeeded, while the excesses committed by mercenary troops, the Mahrattas and Rohillas, who, being mutinous, ill paid, and under no discipline or restraint, and committing all sorts of outrages unpunished, filled up the measure of calamity.

It has been said, that the plunder and the outrages committed by the armies of Nadir Shah, and Ahmed Shah Abdallah, were less destructive than the havoc produced by the lawless wretches whom the degenerate Moghuls were compelled to call in to their assistance against the more warlike race which had established themselves in their neighbourhood: the incursions of these invaders, it has been observed, were like violent tempests which carry every thing before them, but which soon subside; whereas the waste and desolation produced by the Rohillas, resembled pestilential gales, following each other with undiminished fury, and effecting the total destruction of a country exposed to their withering breath. The ruins, which have formed the subject of the accompanying engraving, are situated within a short distance of an old Patan fortress, the palace of Firoze Shah, which, in addition to its own peculiar claims to notice, is in possession of a Hindoo relic, to which considerable interest is attached. The fortress is of great extent, and, amongst other buildings, contains a mosque, erected on the site of a Hindoo temple. In the front of this mosque, in the place where it was first erected, stands a pillar of mixed metal, about twenty-five in height, and embellished with ancient and now unintelligible characters. This column goes by the name of Firoze Shah's Walking Stick.

HURDWAR, A PLACE OF HINDOO PILGRIMAGE.

It is said to have been cast amid spells and incantations, by an ancestor of the Rajah Paitowra, who was assured by the sages and astrologers of his court, that, as long as it continued standing, his children should rule over the inheritance which he bequeatned to them. Upon learning this tradition, Firoze Shah would not proceed in the work of demolition commenced upon the pagoda, but allowed the column to stand in the place where it had been originally erected, in order to shew the fallacy of the prediction. He strewed the pavement around it with the broken idols of Hindoo worship; these have long since turned to dust, but the pillar still remains, a trophy of the victory of the believer over paganism, though no longer the proud emblem of Moslem rule—the feeble representative of this once powerful conqueror being now a tributary to a Christian state. The camp of a British army has been frequently pitched amidst the ruins of Old Delhi; and instances of the mutability of human glory, not less remarkable than that which is perpetuated by Firoze Shah's Walking Stick, have been witnessed amid the fragments of these lonely ruins.

The deliverance of the unfortunate Shah Allum by Lord Lake, in 1803, from the power of the Mahrattas, again changed the destinies of Delhi, which, since that period, has enjoyed unexampled tranquillity. Though the beauty of the scene is diminished, the sublimity of these time and tempest worn ruins is increased by the absence of vegetation on the arid plain on which they stand. The Jumna overflows the country, but its waters, at this place, do not confer fertility, the bed of the river being very strongly impregnated with natron; vegetation is destroyed by the periodical inundations; and, in consequence of the deleterious effects of the floods, and the neglect of the wells, a great part of the country about Delhi is converted into an ocean of sand, through which the camels, plodding their weary way, do not find a bush or a blade of grass. The nature of the soil, and the numberless holes and hiding-places, presented in the crevices and fissures of the ruins, afford abundant harbour for snakes. These and other reptiles may be seen gliding through the broken walls of many a crumbling palace, rearing their crests in the porticos and halls, or basking in the courts and terraces. Wolves and jackalls secrete themselves by day in the vaults and recesses of this deserted city, coming forth at night in packs, and making the walls resound with their hideous yells; and the white vulture keeps lonely ward upon the towers and pinnacles, screaming, as it snuffs its prey in the distance, or as its keen eye follows the track of some disabled animal.

HURDWAR.

The point at which the sacred waters of the Ganges enter the plains of Hindoostan is supposed to be peculiarly holy, and Hurdwar, the gate of Hari, or Vishnoo, has been from time immemorial the resort of Hindoo pilgrims, hurrying to fling themselves into the mighty stream at the moment of its emancipation from the mountain range whence it has its source. The scenery about Hurdwar affords some of the most splendid landscapes which are to be found on the bright and beautiful river, whose majestic course is diversified by so many interesting objects. It stands at the base of a steep mountain, on the verge of a slip of land reclaimed from the forest, and surrounded on all sides by thick jungle. The leafy fastnesses of the Deyrah Dhoon appear immediately above the pass, and, below the uncultivated wastes of the Terraie, stretch their wildernesses for many miles. In the midst of this wild forest scene appear the stately and spacious mansions of rich Hindoos, which recede a little from the river, leaving a handsome esplanade between.

The town is small, but well built; the wealthy portion of the pilgrims only requiring the accommodation of a roof, the remainder of the vast multitude, whom religion, pleasure, or business, bring to the spot, contenting themselves with canvass dwellings, or a bivouac beneath the trees. The annual fair, which attracts this immense concourse of visitors, is held in the month of April; and though spiritual concerns form the ostensible object of the meeting, there is a great admixture of worldly pursuits, even the bathers themselves being intent upon some advantageous bargain in the sale or purchase of the merchandise, which is annually brought to this wild and solitary spot from every part of the world. During the time of the fair, the neighbouring roads are crowded by thousands of travellers in every description of vehicle, mounted upon elephants, bullocks, and camels, on horse-back, or on foot, and of all ages, complexions, and costumes. As they pass the pagodas on their way, the air resounds with the shouts of "Mahadeo Bol!" which is repeated from front to rear, until the distant echoes take up the note, and the welkin rings with the cry of Bol! Bol! Numerous Europeans are induced to visit Hurdwar during the period of its festivity; and their tents and equipages, differing so widely from those of the surrounding multitude, present one of the most extraordinary features of the motley scene. The fair and the ghaut divide the attention of persons whom curiosity merely has drawn to the spot; in the latter, immense crowds succeed each other without intermission, the vast influx of people thronging to the river side, especially at the auspicious moment in which ablution is considered most efficacious, having until lately been productive of very serious accidents. Formerly a narrow avenue led from the principal street to the ghaut; the rush was then tremendous, and numerous lives were lost, not fewer than seven hundred falling a sacrifice in one day to the enthusiastic zeal with which the devotees pressed forward to the river. The road has been widened, and a convenient ghaut constructed, by order of the East India government, and, with the shouts of Mahadao, are now raised acclamations of thanksgiving for the blessing which the pilgrims enjoy, in being able to perform so essential a rite of their religion without danger or difficulty. Brahmins are, of course, amongst the most conspicuous figures in the throng; they collect the tribute, but do not otherwise exercise their sacerdotal character, the bathing being performed without any peculiar ceremony: there are also a vast number of mendicants of every description; many being, from their filth, their distortion, or their nakedness, the most disgusting creatures imaginable. The utter absorption of every faculty in the duty performed by the bathers, who seem to be wholly intent upon saturating themselves with the sacred waters of the Ganges, offers an extraordinary contrast to the idle indifferent air of the European spectators, who, lazily reposing on their elephants, survey the scene at a convenient distance: a few missionaries are more actively employed in distributing copies of the scrip-

TAJ BOWLEE, BEJAPORE.

tures, translated into the various dialects of the East. These are eagerly received even by the most devout followers of Brahma, the Hindoos being exceedingly tolerant of other religions, and ready to listen to their doctrines, although, from the extraordinary influence of caste, the difficulty of making converts is so great, that, were it not for the untiring perseverance of the disciples of Christianity, even the little which is done could not be effected. When tired of gazing upon the assembled thousands, all employed in the same observance, but each Hindoo community differing so strongly from the other, that they scarcely seem to belong to the same clime and country, the idle visitant turns to the fair, where the spectacle is still more diversified, the concourse of men and animals being almost beyond belief. Specimens of the feline race, from the tiger down to the Persian cat, horses, dogs, bears, monkeys, birds, and deer of every description, are offered for sale. The trumpetings of the elephants, the doleful cry of the camels, the lowing of the bullocks, the neighing of the horses, and the shrill screams or sharp roars of beasts and birds of prey, added to the sound of human voices, the discordant notes of itinerant musicians, and the wild blasts from the sacred shells of the Brahmins, altogether make up a concert so confusing and bewildering, that it requires no common strength of nerve to bear it without shrinking. In the booths the precious commodities of the East lie mingled with the manufactures of Europe, hardware, mirrors, woollen cloths, muslins, patent medicines, stationery, and perfumery from France and England, are to be seen by the side of rarities from Cashmere, Persia, the shores of the Red Sea, China, the islands of the Eastern Archipelago, the plains of Tartary, and the heights of the Nepaul. Such goods as are not disposed of at the fair are brought down to the large cities of Hindoostan, to Cawnpore, Allahabad, Benares, and as low as Patna, the last resting-place of the camel.

From the latest accounts from Hindoostan we learn, that, in consequence of the diminished numbers of the pilgrims, the fair is on the decline. The Brahmins of the place, it is said, on the authority of some of the native papers, do not scruple to predict a speedy termination to its sanctity. The falling off from religious zeal is attributed to the intercourse with Europeans, and to the astonishing proofs of their power in the East. It was believed, that while Bhurtpore stood, the English would never gain entire possession of the country; and after its capture, many looked up to Runjeet Singh as the restorer of native supremacy: but the late interview which took place between the Governor-General of India and the sovereign of Lahore, seems to have dissipated this notion. Brahmins also are found to engage more readily in the service of Europeans as Chuprassies and Hurkaras than heretofore; and all over India the religious festivals of the Hindoos are degenerating and falling into contempt.

TAJ BOWLEE, BEJAPORE.

The ruined city which commemorates the short but splendid reign of the Adil Shah dynasty, has been truly and poetically styled the Palmyra of the Deccan. It contains an immense number of buildings, not less interesting than magnificent, which arose and were finished within two hundred years; and which, despite of the desolation which has fallen upon them, still retain a considerable portion of their original beauty. Many have been scarcely injured by the lapse of time, the utter abandonment of man, and the strife of the elements. On approaching from the north, the great dome of Mohammed Shah's tomb first attracts the eye; it is to be seen from the village of Kunnoor, at the distance of fourteen miles; and in drawing nearer, other cupolas, towers, and pinnacles spring up so thickly and so numerously, that it is impossible to banish the expectation of arriving at a populous and still flourishing capital. The road to the outer wall, it is true, leads through ruins; but this is no uncommon circumstance in the environs of Indian cities; and as the guns are still mounted, and the prince to whom it has fallen keeps the ramparts and the gates still manned, the idea is not dispelled until the traveller actually finds himself in the streets, many of which are so choked up with jungle, as to be impassable. It is now a city of tombs, and travellers, wandering through its unbroken solitudes, have remarked the melancholy contrast afforded by the admirable state of repair which distinguishes those edifices, reared in honour of the dead, with the utter demolition of the houses formerly inhabited by the living residents of the city.

The fine reservoir of water, delineated in the accompanying engraving, is situated under the walls, at a short distance from the Mecca gate: it was the work of Mulik Scindal, the friend and favourite of Sultan Mahmoud, the most popular of the Bejapore kings, who commemorated his fidelity to his master, and the superb reward bestowed upon it, by the formation of one of the most splendid tanks which can be found in this part of India. The pond, or bowlee, as it is called, is nearly one hundred yards square, and fifty feet deep: it is surrounded on three sides by a colonnade, with a gallery above; on the fourth, the entrance is through a magnificent archway, flanked by handsome wings, expressly built for the accommodation of travellers. The water is kept very pure, by the few natives who still inhabit the spot; and though sometimes polluted by Christian bathers, the European visitors usually desist from this mode of annoyance, when remonstrated with upon the subject.

At a short distance from the Taj Bowlee, there in another very interesting building, consisting of a mosque and gateway, called the Maitree Kujoos. It is small, but very elegant in its design, and elaborately finished; the material is a fine closely-grained black stone, capable of receiving a high polish; there are three stories in height, and from the angles are attached an embellishment not uncommon in India, consisting of massy stone chains, cut out of solid blocks, there being no joinings perceptible in the links. The story attached to this mosque is rather curious: its founder belonged to the very lowest class of society; an outcast, in fact, who followed an occupation deemed to be of the most degrading nature, and who, especially at the period in which he flourished, could not, in the ordinary course of things, attain either to wealth or consequence; his employment was that of a sweeper, the worst paid, and the most abject menial attached to an Indian establishment. The elevation of this person was owing to an accident, which disconcerted the deep-laid scheme of a pretender to the occult art. Ibrahim Shah the First, having for a long period been afflicted with a distressing malady, and having consulted the medical attendants of his court in vain, sent for an astrologer of some repute, and inquired of him, whether he could procure his restoration to health through the influence of the stars. The

BEJAPORE.

sage, determined that one person, at least, should be benefited by their means, and intending that the luck should fall upon himself, told the king, that the heavenly bodies would prove favourable to his wishes, if, upon a particular morning, he should present a very large sum of money, naming the amount, to the first human being he should see. There is no doubt that the astrologer intended to present his own person to the notice of the king; but Ibrahim, in his anxiety to avail himself of so easy a mode of procuring relief, arose at an unusually early hour, and, proceeding into the court of the palace, was met by a sweeper, a domestic always astir betimes in the morning. The king put the money into the astonished sweeper's hand, who, not coveting wealth for his own use, or perhaps aware, that, cut off as he was from the probability of obtaining respect and distinction, it would be a barren possession, employed it in the erection of a building, which still remains entire, attracting the traveller's eye by the symmetry of its proportions, and the beauty of the carved work with which it is adorned.

BEJAPORE.

It is the custom for travellers, in India, to proceed directly through the city whose outskirts may be selected for the day's halting-place, and to pitch their tents upon the opposite side; thus avoiding the impediments which might retard their progress at the commencement of their journey, were they to be embarrassed by the obstructions of a town. As the gates of Indian cities still continue to be shut at night, there would be difficulty in getting them opened before the usual hour; and this circumstance affords another reason for an arrangement, which enables the traveller to go forward at any period most convenient to himself. The European stranger, on entering Bejapore after a dusty march, is struck, as he passes down the principal street, represented in the accompanying engraving, by a feature always associated in the mind with Oriental architecture, but which is not so frequently met with in India as might be expected,—fountains cooling the air with their crystal waters. Wells and tanks are frequent, but we seldom see such fountains as we have imaged in our minds from the description given in the Arabian Tales, of artificial cascades watering the gardens of Damascus, wooing the traveller by their bubbling melody to refresh his parched lips, and bathe his burning brow. The former sovereigns of Bejapore were not inattentive to this luxury, and, by the side of many ruined houses, the pure element gushes forth from the gaping mouths of sculptured animals, bright, and clear, and beautiful as ever, rejoicing in the sunlight, with the same sweet sound as in those better times when all around was young and vigorous as itself.

To Ally Adil Shah, the fifth monarch of his dynasty, the city of Bejapore is indebted for the aqueducts which convey water throughout the streets; works which are little impaired by time, and, with others still in existence, perpetuate the splendours of his reign. These fountains constitute almost the sole remains of former grandeur in this portion of the city, where the houses are fast verging to the last stages of decay. The building which is seen to the left, however, a portion of the Jumma Musjid, bids fair to survive the ruin which has fallen upon the dwellings of the Omrahs in its neighbourhood.

This superb edifice is also the work of Ally Adil Shah; it is a noble building, having a peculiarity not unfrequent in the mosques of India, that of being entirely open upon one side. The temple is, in fact, composed of rows of arches; these form the entrances which stretch along the whole façade, fronting a spacious quadrangle enclosed all round with a cloister, or piazza, arched in the same manner as the principal building. A large light dome springs from the centre, and the court beyond is embellished by a reservoir and fountain of water. The faithful often perform their orisons by the side of this basin, prostrating themselves upon the ground, and touching the pavement many times with their foreheads. The position of Christian visiters is sometimes rather singular; they may be seen seated at their ease within the sacred precincts of this stately hall, while the devout believer stands at the threshold, and, apparently unconscious of their presence, pours forth his prayers and petitions with all the fervour of devotion. In more populous places than Bejapore, large congregations are only assembled in the mosques upon particular occasions, during the celebration of feasts and festivals. There are pulpits, from which the Moollahs preach, and expound passages from the Koran; but they are not much in use, and, like Zobeide in the city given over to idolatry, we might wander through fifty deserted places of worship without hearing the word of the prophet.

The interior of the Jumma Musjid is very richly ornamented with inscriptions of gold upon lapis lazuli: its interior aspect reminds the spectator of the solemn grandeur of the cathedrals of European countries; the series of arches which succeed, and cross each other, from whatever point of view he may place himself, produces a noble effect of perspective; and the style of its ornaments, which are judiciously, though sparingly, distributed over the walls, is in fine keeping with the remainder of the building, and reflects great honour on the taste of the artist, and that of the prince under whose auspices the work was completed. A few poor priests are still in attendance; but the outer chambers, formerly appropriated to the accommodation of Moollahs, and other holy persons belonging to the mosque, are now inhabited by some of the most disreputable classes of society. Sometimes a momentary gleam of splendour is imparted to the desolate and romantic city of Bejapore, by a visit from one of the present rulers of India. Upon a recent occasion, the honours paid to the governor of Bombay had nearly proved fatal to the mouldering piles tottering to their foundations, and unable to stand against the thunder of artillery.

Amidst the objects of curiosity preserved at Bejapore, is a large gun, formed of mixed metal, of which there is said to be some portion of gold, and a very considerable quantity of silver. The weight is forty tons, and it is allowed to be the largest piece of ordnance of the same description in the world. This splendid gun was the work of Chuleby Roomy Khan, an officer in the service of Hoossein Nizam Shah, at Ahmudnuggur: the mould in which it was cast is still in existence, and lies neglected in the garden of the tomb of the founder, which has been converted into quarters for an English officer. This gun is supposed to have been taken, in 1562, by Ally Adil Shah; and many persons who visit Bejapore, regret that such a splendid specimen of the art of cannon-founding in India, at the distance of three hundred years, should be allowed to remain neglected on the dilapidated walls of a city so little known as Bejapore, instead of being placed in some

SULTAN MAHOMED SHAHS TOMB, BEJAPORE.

conspicuous situation in England, where it would attract the admiration of the whole of Europe. Others are of opinion, that we should commit an act more worthy of a despot than a generous conqueror, in adorning our capital with the spoils of foreign countries; and are better pleased that the gun should remain surrounded by buildings coeval with itself, and associated with its history. There can be no doubt that the loss of this gun would inflict the deepest sorrow and mortification upon the native inhabitants of Bejapore, who, both Moslem and Hindoo, approach it with great reverence, paying almost divine honours to a power which inspires them with awe and veneration. It is styled Mulki Meidan, or Moolk e Meidan, sovereign of the plain; and English officers visiting Bejapore, have seen with surprise the native advance towards it with joined hands, and devotion in their countenances. One of these gentlemen observes, that white flowers were strewed on the bore, the forepart of the muzzle was smeared with cinnabar and oil, and there were marks as well as odours of lately-burned perfumes, which plainly indicated that an offering had been made to the spirit residing in this warlike shrine. The gun is enriched with inscriptions and devices, in the florid style which characterizes Oriental embellishments of this nature: the portions not thus ornamented, present a surface so smooth and polished as to be absolutely slippery; and the sonorous sound of the metal proves the large proportion of silver of which it is composed. It is a common practice among young European officers, to effect an entrance through the mouth of this enormous piece of ordnance, the interior being furnished with a seat for their accommodation: it will contain five persons without much crowding; but the occupants, while enjoying themselves in their shady retreat, are often ejected by a very summary process. Some mischievous wight on the outside, moves the rings, striking them against the gun. The sound produced is tremendous, and the vibrations so distressing, that out come the whole party as if they were shot. On the visit of Sir John Malcolm, during the period of his viceroyship at Bombay, the Satara Rajah, who holds the surrounding territories under the British government, directed that this gun should be fired off as an appropriate salute. Though not charged with more than half the weight of powder which its chamber could contain, the concussion was awful; it shook many of the buildings to their foundations, and the terrified inhabitants, as the reverberations rolled along, expected to see the domes and towers, survivors of former shocks, come tumbling about their ears. It is said by the natives, that Moolk e Meidan had a sister of similar size, named Kurk o Budglee, thunder and lightning, and that it was carried to Poonah. No trace, however, remains of this less fortunate twin; if it ever existed, which is doubtful, it must have been melted down long ago. A model of the sovereign of the plain has been brought to England, and forms a part of a very noble collection of curiosities in the possession of an officer of the Bombay army.

TOMB OF MAHOMED SHAH.

The Burra Gumbooz, great dome, as it is called by the natives, which surmounts the massive tomb of the most popular monarch of the Adil Shah dynasty, forms the principal attraction of a city full of wonders. Mahomed Shah was the last independent sovereign of Bejapore; he came to the throne at a very early age, when he was not more than sixteen, and found a large treasury, a country still flourishing, and a well-appointed army, reported to be two hundred and eighty thousand strong.

The taste for useless splendour and posthumous fame, so remarkably exemplified in the tombs of Hindoostan, is displayed in the fullest extent in the mausoleum of Mahomed Shah, which was constructed in the life-time of the monarch, and under his own auspices. Though somewhat heavy and cumbrous in its structure, its amazing size, and the symmetry of its proportions, fill the mind with reverential feelings: from whatsoever point it is surveyed, whether near or at a distance, its surpassing magnitude reduces all the surrounding objects to comparative insignificance, while its grave and solemn character assimilates very harmoniously with the desolate grandeur of the ruins which it overtops.

The Burra Gumbooz, which is visible from every point of the adjacent country, exceeds the dome of St. Paul's in diameter, and is only inferior to that of St. Peter's at Rome. It crowns a quadrangular stately building, consisting of a single hall, one hundred and fifty feet square, and, including the cupola, upwards of a hundred and fifty feet in height. There are four octagonal towers, one at each angle, each is surmounted by a dome, and contains a spiral staircase by which the ascent to the roof may be made: though there is more of *apparent* solidity than of elegance in this building, its ornaments are rich and appropriate, none are introduced which could injure its simplicity; and, altogether, there are few of the Moslem remains in India more striking or splendid than the sepulchre of Mahomed Shah. Unfortunately, the prodigious weight of the dome, and possibly the badness of the foundation, have reduced the whole fabric to a state of general decay; an officer, visiting Bejapore a few years ago, reports that the primary walls are not only split in some places through and through, but also in a parallel direction to their faces, so that in all probability, and at no distant period, the whole will come instantaneously to the ground. The tomb is raised upon a terrace of granite two hundred yards square; below are many gloomy chambers, now almost choked up with rubbish, but the quadrangle in front of the main building is well kept, and adorned with fountains; and on the western side there is a second terrace, leading to a mosque corresponding in form with the mausoleum, but accompanied by two slight and elegant minars, which give grace and lightness to the whole. The sarcophagus of Mahomed Shah is placed upon a raised platform of granite, under a wooden canopy in the centre of the hall; on his right, are the tombs of his son and his daughter-in-law; on the left, those of a favourite dancing girl, his daughter, and his wife: the whole are covered with holy earth brought from Mecca, mixed with sandal-wood dust; but although this sort of plastering may excite the admiration of the devout disciples of the prophet, it gives the monuments a very mean appearance; the canopy over that of Mahomed Shah is said to have been of solid silver, but, having fallen a prey to the rapacity of the Mahrattas, a shrine of humbler materials was substituted. The surrounding walls are embellished with inscriptions from the Koran, in alto relievo; the characters being gilded and raised upon a deep blue ground of enamel, formed by a liquid coating of lapis lazuli; the gold ornaments beautifully interwoven together, and embossed upon this splendid material, produce a very fine effect, and are introduced with great judgment.

The present inhabitants of Bejapore retain a more lively recollection of Mahomed Shah than of any of his predecessors; he is represented to have been a prince of peculiarly amiable character, and to have possessed those virtues most in esteem amongst Asiatics: he is extolled for his wisdom, his justice, and, above all, for his munificence; and though the circumstance of his being the last independent prince of Bejapore may account for the glory which encircles his name, as he was also the best known of all the princes of the Adil Shah dynasty, we may suppose that he really merited the commendations which are lavished upon his memory. During the whole of his reign, he kept up a good understanding with the Moghul emperor, Shah Jehan, whom he courted through the medium of his favourite son, Dara. The intimacy and confidence which existed between the sovereign of Bejapore and this unfortunate prince, excited the jealousy of Aurungzebe, who, independent of his ambitious desire to bring all the Mahommedan kingdoms of India under his own sway, entertained a personal hatred to those monarchs who espoused the interests of his brother; and the enmity thus drawn upon Bejapore, was openly displayed at the first convenient opportunity. Mohamed at his death was succeeded by his son Ali Adil Shah II., at this time nineteen years of age. The resources of the country were still considerable; he had a well-filled treasury, a fertile territory, and his army, had it been properly concentrated, was powerful. The troops unfortunately were greatly divided, large bodies being employed in reducing the refractory Zemindars of the Carnatic. Ali Adil Shah mounted the throne without any complimentary reference, or the observance of the homage which Aurungzebe pretended to claim by right of an admission from Mahomed Shah. The Moghuls immediately gave out that he was not the son of the late king, and that it was incumbent upon the emperor to nominate a successor. "This war," observes the historian, "upon the part of the Moghuls, appears to have been more completely destitute of apology than any that is commonly found even in the unprincipled transactions of Asiatic governments." It is said, that, on the final reduction of Bejapore, the conqueror received a severe reproof from the lips of his favourite daughter. Boasting of the success with which Providence had crowned his arms in every quarter, and of his having, by the extinction of this sovereignty, accomplished all the objects of his ambition, and subdued and dethroned every powerful king throughout Hindoostan and the Deccan, the Begum observed, "Your Majesty, it is true, is the conqueror of the world; but you have departed from the wise policy of your illustrious ancestors, who, when they subdued kingdoms, made the possessors of them their subjects and tributaries, and thus became king of kings, while you are now only a simple monarch, without royal subjects to pay you homage." Aurungzebe, we are told, was forcibly struck with the justice of this remark, which occasioned him so much uneasiness, that he could not refrain from expressing his displeasure at the delivery of sentiments so mortifying to his vanity.

GRASS ROPE BRIDGE AT TEREE,—PROVINCE OF GURWALL.

Suspension bridges formed of grass ropes, the simple, useful, and elegant invention of the rude mountaineers of the Himalaya, are of considerable antiquity in the provinces where they are found: they are said to have given the original hint to the chain bridges of Europe, and to those which Mr. Shakespeare has constructed so much to the public advantage in India. The bridge of Teree affords a very beautiful specimen of its class; the adjacent scenery, and the rocky rampart on either side of the river, adding considerably to its picturesque effect. In some of the hill districts, where the natural advantages of the country are not so great, the bridge is suspended from scaffolds erected on both banks of the stream, over these are stretched ropes of great thickness, to afford on each side a support for the flooring, if it may be so called, which is formed of a ladder wattled with twigs and branches of trees, and attached to the balustrade by pendent ropes. The main ropes are extremely slack, and, where the banks are not very high, the centre of the bridge is within a foot of the water; but even at this altitude the danger of immersion would be very great, since the current of these mountain streams runs with such rapidity, that the best swimmer would find considerable difficulty in effecting a safe landing.

The province of Gurwall is situated between the 30th and 31st degrees of north latitude; it is bounded on the north by the snowy range of the Himalaya, and on the south by the great plain of the Ganges: the rivers which form the source of the Ganges run to the east, and the Jumna pursues its course along the western frontier. The province chiefly consists of an assemblage of hills, heaped confusedly together in many forms and directions, sometimes in chains lying parallel to each other but of no great extent, and often connected at their termination by narrow ridges. There is a very striking diversity in the shape of these hills and the distance between each range is exceedingly circumscribed, consequently the valleys are narrow and confined, not a spot is to be seen which would afford room for an encampment of a thousand men. Some of these ranges are covered with wood, and present a scene of perpetual verdure; the arbutus and other flowering trees attain to great perfection, and the polyandria monogynia, which grows to forty feet in height, loads the air with the perfume of its multitudinous blossoms. In other places, ridges of bare rock are piled upon each other, and the whole is wild, broken, and overrun with jungle. There is of course little cultivation, and the revenues of the province have always been been very trifling.

We are told by a writer upon the subject, that the district, in consequence of its poverty, was for many years exempted from tribute. Acbar, however, not willing that any of his neighbours should escape, demanded from the chief an account of the revenues of his raje, and a chart of the country. The rajah being then at court, repaired to the presence the following day, and, in obedience to the imperial command, presented a true but not very tempting report of the state of his finances, and, as a correct representative of the chart of his country, facetiously introduced a lean camel, saying, "This is a faithful picture of the teritory I possess—up and down, and very poor." The emperor smiled at

GRASS ROPE BRIDGE AT TEREE. — GURWALL.

the ingenuity of the device, and told him, that from the revenue of a country realized with so much labour, and in amount so small, he had nothing to demand. Subsequently on the invasion of the Ghorkas, a tribute of twenty-five thousand rupees annually was exacted. These people, under an able leader, Ammeer Singh, stretched their conquests to the British frontier, and, after considerable difficulty, were at length dislodged by Sir David Ochterlony, whose skill and conduct retrieved the fortunes of the war, which until he assumed the command, had declared in favour of the enemy.

The neighbourhood of Gurwall abounds with game of many descriptions. Elephants are found amid its fastnesses, and sometimes make incursions beyond their native woods, to the great injury of whatever they may meet with, but their depredations are particularly directed towards the sugar plantations. They are considered inferior in size and value to the elephants brought from the eastern countries, and are seldom caught, except for the purpose of taking their teeth: the common mode is by pit-falls, but they are also driven from their haunts in the forest, and surrounded by troops of professed hunters, brought up from their infancy to the chase. Rhinoceroses, wild buffaloes, and many kinds of deer inhabit these districts; while, farther up in the hills, there are traditions of the existence of the unicorn, which sometimes beguile English officers of their night's rest, employed in anxious vigils to obtain a sight of so extraordinary an animal. Birds are very numerous, and very beautiful: the pheasant, which does not visit the plains of India, occurs in great variety amid the ranges of the hills; the spotted, the speckled, the golden, or burnished, and the argus-eyed, build on the leafy coverts of the woods. Of the latter kind one species are of a light blue colour, and another brown, both have the eyes beautifully delineated at the extremity of the feathers. The great dainty of an Indian table, the florikin, also rewards the sportsman's toil; black partridge, hares, and quail are plentiful; they may be shot without much labour; and the eager pursuer who does not consider the ascending of the heights and creeping into jungles material obstacles to his amusement, will find two species of fowls, and the deer called parah by the natives, the cervus porcinus of Linnæus.

The nullahs are full of fish, and the methods pursued by the natives in taking them are very curious; sometimes a rod and line are used, but in a very different way from that employed in angling in Europe. About ten yards of one end of the line is furnished with nooses or snares from one to three and four hairs strong, according to the size of the fish which is expected to be caught, and ranged at intervals about fifteen inches apart: oblong pieces of iron, placed in a particular manner, prevent this simple piece of machinery from being carried away by the force of the current. The other end of the line, consisting of ten or twelve yards, is passed through a bow at the end of a short rod, and kept in the hand below, and both are managed in the same manner as a trowling rod and line; thus prepared, the fisherman casts the end with the snare across the stream, where he lets it remain about half a minute, during which time he plunges a light forked stick into the holes and recesses of the rocky bed, thus driving the fish up the stream against the snares of the line: three or four fish are usually secured each time, and half an hour suffices to furnish a meal.

Another method practised by the natives is, to stupify the fish with a vegetable substance; for this purpose, they make choice of a pool formed by the current, and, turning the stream by heaping up stones, stop the supply of fresh water by closing every outlet; then bruising the root of a tree common in the neighbourhood, they cast a sufficient quantity into the pool, and in about half an hour its deleterious effect seldom fails to show itself,—the fish, unable to preserve their equilibrium, tumble about, rise to the surface of the water, and are easily taken by the hand.

Teree is a small insignificant place, distinguished only by its scenery, and the bridge which throws its graceful festoon over the rapid and rock-bound stream below. The ropes of this bridge are constructed from the long coarse grass which grows on the sides of the hills; each is about the size of a small hawser, and formed with three strands; they are obliged to be renewed constantly, and, even when in their best condition, the passage across is rather a nervous undertaking. Some very melancholy accidents have occurred to European visiters upon the fragile bridges of the hills, but, with increasing communication, doubtless a better mode of transit will be adopted.

DHER WARRA,—CAVES OF ELLORA.

At the southern extremity of the excavations of Ellora, these sublime works are terminated by a large cave, less richly ornamented than the more celebrated portions of the series, but rendered very imposing from its size, and the splendid row of columns with which it is supported on either side.

It is said that it derives the name of Dher Warra from its having been the temple of the Dhairs, a low and impure caste; and so great is the native prejudice against it, that the Brahmins not only object to enter themselves, but remonstrate with the European visitants on the degradation which they must incur in treading the polluted haunt. The name of this cavern, and its supposed dedication to the Dhairs, are both of modern origin; like many others in Ellora, it is a temple of Boodh, whose statue and attributes appear in the same manner as in the Bisma Kurm, and other acknowledged Boodh temples. The principal hall, represented in the engraving, is about a hundred feet long, and forty in breadth, not including the recesses, of which there is one on either side. The pillars supporting the roof are slighter and more elegant than those of the other caves; and it is further distinguished by two platforms slightly elevated from the ground, which traverse the whole length of the excavation, and are supposed to have been intended for the accommodation of students, scribes, or the venders of merchandise. The traffic carried on by the Hindoos, who are notoriously a money-getting race, at all convenient opportunities, and the fairs which they are accustomed to hold during the celebration of their religious festivals, render the latter supposition very probable. The cave is commodiously situated for such a purpose, and the facility of egress and regress has rendered it a favourite asylum for cattle and goats. The dirt which these animals occasion, and the multitude of all sorts of insects which they attract, have doubtless been partly the cause of the ill name which has been bestowed upon the cave, and the notion that it is only fit for the abode of scavengers.

INTERIOR OF DHER WARRA. CAVES OF ELLORA.

TOMB OF IBRAHIM PADSHAH.—BEJAPORE.

The front of the Dher Warra is open to the country; and though there is no exterior ornament, some gigantic sitting figures, at the entrance of the smallest of the series, have a very striking effect, and give to the visiter approaching on that side a true notion of the splendour which a nearer inspection of the range will afford. There are colossal figures standing in niches or shrines at the extremity of the Dher Warra, but the roof is without any ornament; yet though so little indebted to the sculptor, compared to the elaborate embellishments of others of the neighbouring excavations, few persons can stand at the entrance, and survey the grand dimensions of its interior without the strongest feeling of gratification, while the view which it affords is both beautiful and extensive. The waters of a nullah divide it from the Bisma Kurm: the temple stands upon a commanding height, having in front a plain of gentle acclivity, not much overrun with brushwood, and diversified by a few single trees, of noble growth and luxuriant foliage.

TOMB OF IBRAHIM PADSHAH, BEJAPORE.

About half a mile to the northward of Bejapore, in the garden of the twelve Imaums, the Durga of Abou al Muzzaffir, as the natives term the majestic tomb of Ibrahim Adil Shah II. rises with a pomp of architecture exceeding even the magnificence of the buildings in its neighbourhood. The great and amiable sovereign who sleeps within this noble pile, is represented by Ferishta, his contemporary, as having been one of the brighest ornaments of royalty; his virtues still live in the memory of the people of the Deccan; and, to this day, the ashes of the good and great, the parent, the instructor, and the friend, are visited with equal reverence and delight by the Mussulman, the Hindoo, and the Christian traveller.

This splendid mausoleum was built under the direction of Mulick Secunder, or, as he is sometimes called, Mulik Scindal, who is said to have constructed the Taj Bowlee at his own expense. According to report, it was commenced in the reign of Ibrahim, and intended as the tomb of his beloved daughter, Zoran Sultan, who died at the age of six years, and whose infant virtues are commemorated in a Persian inscription. The death of the monarch who planned the design, in all its grand and beautiful proportions, took place before it was completed, and he lies interred amid the members of his family, in the mausoleum of the garden, which gave its name to the neighbouring entrance of the city, formerly called the Imaums, but now known as the Mecca-gate.

The style of Ibrahim Shah's tomb differs entirely from that of the Burra Gumbooz, illustrated in a preceding plate, bearing a stronger resemblance to the generality of the Durgas, seen in Hindoostan. It consists of a mosque and mausoleum, raised upon the same platform, both of which are represented in the accompanying engraving. The basement of these superb edifices is one hundred and thirty yards in length, and fifty-two in breadth, rising to the height of fifteen feet, and enclosed by buildings of a single story, open both from without and within, and intended for the accommodation of visiters, travellers, and the attendants of the place. The entrance to the interior quadrangle which is seen to the right of the plate, is on the north side, by a lofty and elegant gateway, flanked by tall minarets of exquisite grace and lightness. This portal leads to a handsome flight of steps, and through another gate of a new construction, up to the raised terrace, on which the mosque and the place of sepulchre stand. The sarcophaguses of the king and his family are placed in a large hall in the centre of the building; this hall is enclosed by an outer and inner veranda—the first thirteen feet broad, and twenty-two high; the outer, twenty feet by thirty, supported by seven arches on each face. The dome above is raised on arches, five in the long curtain face, and three in the depth; a staircase leads to a flat terrace, spreading above the veranda, and from the minarets at each corner, a lofty balustraded wall, richly ornamented, extends along every side; a second balustrade, of similar proportions, a flight of steps higher up, forms a spacious balcony round the base of the dome; it is finished in the same style of elegance and splendour with corresponding minarets at the angles, differing only from those below in their height, as will be seen in the engraving. The dome is thirty-five feet in diameter but, unlike that of the Jumma Musjid, it has the shape of a segment of a globe cut through one-third part of its perpendicular axis. This form is airy and elegant, but would be difficult to execute upon a large scale, owing to the narrow span of its aperture, and the great exterior flexure of the curve which overhangs its base. A column rises on the summit of the dome, crowned with a crescent.

The simplicity of the central hall, which contains the monumental remains of the king and his family, forms a striking contrast to the splendour of embellishment lavished on the exterior; yet its ornaments are not less effective, or worthy of admiration. It is forty feet square, and thirty high, and the walls are of such finely grained black granite, as to have been mistaken for marble. The ceiling is particularly fine, the whole roof being formed of the same kind of stone; and, as it is asserted, without the slighest admixture of timber. This ceiling is so constructed, that it does not appear to rest upon the main walls of the building, but on a cornice projected from them, so that the area is reduced from forty to twenty-two feet on each side. The roof is quite flat, and richly ornamented, being divided into square compartments; the traverses of which, though of several pieces, look like solid beams; and it excites wonder that a heavy mass, so disposed, should have existed so many years without the slightest derangement of its parts. The death of Ibrahim Adil Shah took place in A. D. 1626; his sepulchre must therefore be at least two hundred years old; the building being commenced in his life-time, and only occupying twelve years. The interstices of the stones on the top of the arches, in the surrounding verandas, are filled with lead, and clamped together by ponderous bars of iron, some of which have been wrenched from their places by the destructive Mahrattas, who probably expected to find some rich treasure concealed there.

The verandas and the walls are ornamented with beautiful sculpture, chiefly from the Koran, the whole of which is said to be carved on the several compartments. The inscriptions are raised in the manner of basso relievo, and so highly polished as to shine like glass. On the northern side the letters are given a greater degree of prominence, by being gilt, and embossed on a blue enamelled ground, adorned with flowers; and the whole has been compared to the illuminations of an Oriental MS. seen through a magnifying glass, and adding the beauties of sculpture to those of painting. The doors, which are the only specimens of woodwork used in the building, are exceedingly handsome, and studded with gilt knobs; the doorways, on either side, are adorned with a great variety of ornaments, beautifully executed; there are windows on each side of the doors, which are four in number; these, and the arches above, are formed of a singular stone lattice-work, composed of Arabic sentences, instead of the ordinary pattern of similar perforations; the light that they admit, proceeding through the verandas, is not very strong, and the whole of the hall is characterized by a gloomy solemnity, in fine keeping with the last resting-place of the dead, but not usually a concomitant of Indian sepulchres.

The sarcophaguses lie north and south; the first contains the body of Hajee Burra Sahib, the Padshah's mother; next her, Taj Sultan, his queen; thirdly, the king himself; on his left, Zoran Sultan, the beloved daughter to whom the building was originally dedicated. Boran Shah, the youngest son of Ibrahim, lies interred by the side of this lamented infant; and beyond, at the furthest extremity, Shah Inshah, the monarch's eldest son. The canopies of these tombs, in which Moslems usually expend such lavish sums, are of tattered silk, scarcely leaving a remnant of original magnificence; a circumstance to be accounted for by the small number and the distressed condition of the followers of the Prophet in the neighbourhood.

The gallery on the veranda which surrounds this hall, is remarkable on account of its stone roof, which is most tastefully sculptured. It is divided into compartments, oblong and square, one hundred and forty-four in number, very few of which have the same ornaments. Each division is formed of a single stone, and exhibits an elegant combination of arabesques in flowers and wreathes, in those fanciful and spirited designs in which Indian artists excel, and which are of so truly Oriental a character. Imagination has here shewn how rich and exhaustless are its stores; and these exquisite delineations are executed with the same masterly power exhibited in the grouping and combination of the endless variety of interwoven garlands. One of the cross stones which support the roof of the veranda against the north face, was struck by a cannon-ball during the last siege of Bejapore. The shot is stated to have been fired from the Moolk e Meidan, the enormous gun mentioned in a preceding page, which seems not improbable, as the mausoleum lies within the range of that extraordinary piece of ordnance. The stone, though split at both ends, and hanging only by the pressure of a single inch against the lower part of the splinter, which holds fast in the cornice, has remained in that position, to the amazement of all who have observed its precarious tenure, since the year 1685, without yielding in the least degree to the effects of gravity.

The mosque which fronts this splendid mausoleum at the distance of forty yards, having a piece of water and a fountain between, is a plain building, one hundred and fifteen feet by seventy-six, crowned with a dome, and flanked at the angles of each story with slender and lofty minarets. The stones of both these buildings are so neatly put together, that it is scarcely possible to perceive where they are joined; and the whole pile, notwithstanding the absence of the white marble which adds such brilliant splendour to the mausoleums of Hindoostan, may vie in magnificence with the most celebrated shrines of

Eastern monarchs. The attendants at the tomb of Ibrahim Padshah are poor, and few in number, owing the income allotted for their subsistence entirely to the bounty of the present rulers of the city. About three thousand five hundred rupees are annually distributed, from the revenues of the district, amongst the Mohammedan attendants at the different tombs and mosques: this, says our authority, "will be considered rather a liberal allowance from a Hindoo government, for the maintenance of a religious class of persons of a different persuasion." The direction of a part of the revenues of the country, for the support of men devoting themselves to the care of tombs and sepulchres, affords one of many proofs of the extraordinary reverence with which the dead are regarded throughout the whole continent of India.

Ibrahim Adil Shah II. seems to have merited the encomiums of an historian, not more remarkable for his attachment to the friend and patron, from whose favour he derived so much honour and advantage, than for the independence of his spirit and the boldness with which he narrates circumstances which a more time-serving courtier would have suppressed altogether. The reign of Ibrahim is not without its blots, but they are few in number, and not of so deep a dye as those which usually stain the annals of Eastern despots. He was tolerant in his religious principles; and though, upon his accession to power, his court shewed their readiness to adopt the opinions professed by the sovereign, whether Soonee or Sheeah, he left every one to follow the dictates of his own conscience, and both sects were allowed to practise their religious ceremonies unmolested.

PERAWA.

The province of Malwa has been less visited and described by the traveller and the historian than any other part of India. Sir John Malcolm, in his memoir of the Central Provinces, tells us that its annals are still involved in darkness and fable; and the short and meagre notices which have hitherto appeared concerning the towns and cities of its districts, afford very unsatisfactory information respecting its present condition. Perawa is an irregular and meanly built town, about seventy miles distant to the north of Oojein, the capital of the province; it is a place of no importance, surrounded by a decayed wall of mud and brick-work, so weak and dilapidated as scarcely to oppose a barrier to the incursions of cattle. The principal building is an old stone fort, represented in the accompanying engraving, which, though not boasting much architectural splendour, is in the highest degree picturesque, and affords a very fair specimen of the edifices of the same nature continually encountered in the wildest and most remote places of India. The style of this fortress is partly Mohammedan and partly Hindoo; the ghaut, with its open pavilions to the left of the plate, affording a pleasing contrast to the bastioned walls of the citadel; it leads to a gateway, which, though it will not bear any comparison to the noble entrances of many of the places of arms in India, is not destitute of architectural beauty.

PERAWA.—MALWA.

The unsettled state of provinces continually at war with each other, and exposed to the incursions of military free-booters of every description, rendered these fortresses of great importance to princes and rulers, frequently compelled to take shelter within their walls, and to defend them against an armed force. Many were strong enough to resist the ineffective weapons of native warfare, but, with the exception of Gwalior, Bhurtpore, and a few other strongly fortified places, few could withstand the power of European ordnance: the princes of Malwa, however inclined to turbulence, are held in subjection by the military force stationed at Mhow, and it is not likely that the fort of Perawa will ever reassume its warlike character.

Malwa is a very fruitful province; its soil consists principally of a black vegetable mould, which in the rainy season becomes so soft as to render travelling hardly practicable; on drying, it cracks in all directions, and the fissures in many parts of the road-side are so wide and deep, that the traveller quitting the beaten track is exposed to some peril, for a horse, getting his foot into one of these fissures, endangers his own limbs and the life of his rider. A large quantity of grain of various kinds is raised by the husbandmen, together with the sugar-cane, tobacco, cotton, linseed, garlic, turmeric, and ginger. The quantity of rain which falls in ordinary seasons is so considerable, and the ground so retentive of moisture, that wells are not resorted to for the purpose of irrigation; thus a great portion of the labour necessary in other parts of Hindoostan is saved. But this advantage is counterbalanced by the greater severity of suffering, upon a failure of the periodical rains; for the husbandman, accustomed to depend upon the spontaneous bounty of Heaven, is with difficulty brought to undertake the unusual labour of watering his fields, especially as it must be preceded by that of digging the wells.

Malwa is celebrated for its grapes; during the rainy season the vines produce a second crop, which is, however, acidulous, and inferior in flavour to the first: the quantity reared is so great, as to supply the bazaars of Indore; the other fruits are, the mango, guava, plantain, melon and water-melon, several varieties of orange and lime trees, from which the natives make a very refreshing sherbet, and as a rarity, in a few gardens, the *casica papyra.* Indigo and the morinda citrifolia, a red-dye plant, is cultivated in small quantities; but the most celebrated product of Malwa is its opium, which is held in particular estimation by the Chinese, who assert that it contains two-sevenths more of pure opium than an equal quantity of the Patna and Benares drug. The poppy, which is sown in November or December, flowers in February; and the opium is extracted in March or April, sooner or later, according to the time of sowing. The white kind yields a larger quantity than the red, but the quality is the same from both. When the flowers have fallen off, and the capsules assume a whitish colour, it is time to wound them. This is done by drawing an instrument with three teeth, at the distance of about half a line from each other, along the capsule, from top to bottom, so as to penetrate the skin. These wounds are made in the afternoon and evening, and the opium is gathered the next morning. The labourers begin at daybreak, and continue until noon. The wounds on each capsule are repeated for three succeeding days; and the whole of the field is completed, and the opium gathered, in fifteen. In a plentiful season, and good ground,

P

from six to nine seers of opium may be obtained from a bigah of land: the seer is equal to two pounds, and the bigah to about a third part of an acre, but both vary in different provinces; in Malwa the seer is reckoned at eighty rupees weight, and the bigah at a hundred square cubits in measurement. In some districts the opium is adulterated with oil, to the amount of a third, or even half, of the whole mass: the practice is avowed, and the reason assigned is, to prevent the drug from drying; in adulterations that are secret, and considered fraudulent, the leaves of the poppy, dried and powdered, are added to the opium. In thinning a piece of ground under cultivation, the very young plants are used as potherbs; but when they attain to a foot and a half in height, their intoxicating quality renders them unfit for such a purpose.

Early in the thirteenth century, Malwa was either entirely conquered, or rendered tributary to the Patan sovereigns of Delhi; it was afterwards erected into an independent kingdom by the Afghauns, a tribe of the same race, who fixed their capital at Mandoo; but it did not long maintain its supremacy, becoming subject to the Moghuls, and continuing to be attached to that empire until the death of Aurungzebe. The Mahratta power then prevailed, and during a long series of years its possession was disputed by different chieftains, whose conflicts enabled others less formidable to invade, plunder, and assume almost regal sway over the villages which their armed followers were strong enough to keep in subjection. A country so fitted for their production, was the birth-place of the Pindarries, which in the first instance consisted of bands of mercenary troops attached to the service of the Peishwa, and, after his withdrawal from the field, thrown upon the public for subsistence. The contributions which they levied in the neighbouring states rendered the occupation popular with idle depraved men of all castes and religions, who crowded to the banner of chieftains assuming the command. This force at length became so formidable, and its devastations so extensive, that the British government felt called upon to interfere. The Bengal army took the field against it, and, after some severe campaigns, succeeded in restoring, or rather, giving tranquillity to the central provinces of India, for, until the period in which Sir John Malcolm was sent to legislate in the disturbed districts, short truces had been the only intervals of peace which they had ever known.

RUINS ON THE BANKS OF THE JUMNA.

The character of the river Jumna differs widely from that of the Ganges, and its scenery is by many travellers considered more picturesque. Its banks are distinguished by multitudes of ruins in the last stages of desolation, the crowds upon the ghauts are less numerous, many splendid specimens of Oriental architecture in these striking landing-places, being wholly unfrequented, or occupied by a few solitary bathers; every cliff is crowned with the remnants of a fortress; and castles and temples, all bearing marks of decay, give to the sandy wilderness a solemn and melancholy air. The mosque represented in the accompanying engraving occurs on the west bank of the Jumna, a short distance from the walls at the upper part of the modern city of Delhi. The cupolas and

A RUIN ON THE BANKS OF THE JUMNA, ABOVE THE CITY OF DELHI.

the gateway, which are still entire, possess strong claims to admiration, and, though upon a much smaller scale than the magnificent remains in the neighbourhood, afford a very just idea of the beauties common to nearly all the places of Mohammedan worship in India. The picturesque effect of these ruins is much heightened by the feathery foliage of the adjoining grove; a graceful accessory, rare in the immediate vicinity of Delhi, where the soil is barren, and remarkable for its saline efflorescence. The rocky ground being always exposed to the rays of the sun, absorbs much heat, and produces a high, dry temperature in the hot season; while, from the openness of the country and its exposure to winds which pass over extensive lakes in the neighbourhood, the winter is proportionably cold. But while these causes operate to prevent the spontaneous vegetation which in other districts arrives at the richest luxuriance without care or culture, they are rather favourable to the labours of the husbandman and the gardener, who are enabled to produce plants common to the warmer parts of India, but which are not found in the upper portion of the great plain spreading to the Himalaya.

The grove which shades this venerable and time-worn mosque was, in all probability, planted by the founder; for a moslem, when building a temple or a monument, always takes the comforts of travellers into consideration. Attached to each, there are generally apartments for the accommodation of casual sojourners; and a well, or tank, shaded by a grove of trees, is the usual accompaniment of these hospitable edifices. The religious tenets both of the Mohammedan and the Hindoo inculcate the social virtues; they deem it very meritorious to appropriate their wealth to useful works, for the benefit of their fellow-creatures: the climate suggests the most effectual means for the performance of this duty; for what can be more welcome and necessary than shelter from the scorching heat of an Eastern sun, or water to allay the raging tortures of thirst? The hot weather is unaccountably chosen, by persons who have long distances to perform, for the commencement of their journeys: the season is generally considered healthy to those who do not expose themselves to fatigue during the sultry hours of the day; but many perish from thirst and weariness, some dropping on the road-side, others reaching the wells only to die at the moment in which their delusive hopes are upon the eve of fulfilment.

The whole of the neighbourhood of Delhi is strewed with the fragments of ruined tombs, temples, serais, and palaces: jheels of water and swamps have formed themselves in the hollowed foundations of the prostrate edifices, adding to the wildness and dreariness of the scene. After traversing these dismal wastes, it is delightful to emerge upon the banks of the Jumna, and to gaze upon its cool waters: the beauty of the landscape here delineated, being much enhanced when these dark ruins intercept the bright silvery light of a full-orbed moon, shining in virgin majesty over plain, and grove, and gently-gliding river. The banks of the Jumna are the haunt of alligators, many of which are of the most dangerous kind, and are known to attack man. These huge monsters lie basking upon the sandy islets which rise above the stream, and seem to be little disturbed by the passing and repassing of the boats, which frequently come down in large fleets, laden with cotton. The quills of the porcupine are scattered on the shore; and there also may be seen the foot-prints of large animals, bears and hyenas, or the animals themselves, stealing with stealthy pace from the neighbouring ravines. Immense numbers of aquatic birds, storks, and gigantic cranes stalk along the shores, float upon the waters, or rise with a wild rush of wings upon the least alarm. As the habitations of man become scarce, animal life seems more abundant; the places of flocks and herds, which in the thickly-peopled portions of the districts through which the Jumna flows are prodigious, are supplied by the untamed tenants of the waste, birds in particular. These last are countless; and the animation which they give to the scene, is so much in accordance with its desert air, as scarcely to enliven the profound solitude which is its prevailing characteristic.

The establishment of a new presidency at Agra, and the successful employment of steam-navigation, will effect a material alteration in the aspect of the Jumna below the capital of Hindoostan Proper, a tract which only comprehends the upper provinces of India; but a very long period must still elapse, before the lonely site of these crumbling ruins can be divested of its savage grandeur. The river is here very shallow in the cold season; during the rains, it comes down in a flood, almost equal in volume to that of the Ganges; but at other periods of the year it is easily fordable, and not navigable for boats of any burden; the water flowing over a rocky bed, is remarkably clear, and, even after its junction with the Ganges, it preserves its pellucid character; the blue stream of the more translucent river being plainly discernible to a considerable distance, amid the turbid waters of its muddy rival. Many of the pebbles which are gathered on the banks of the Jumna afford interesting geological specimens; and some are thought worthy of being polished and worked up into ornamental appendages.

FRONT VIEW OF THE BISMA KURM,—CAVES OF ELLORA.

Early travellers visiting the excavated temples of the islands of Bombay, more struck with horror at the abominations of idolatry, than with admiration of the magnitude of the undertaking and the splendour of the execution, have described them as being "devilish and frightful to view." The caves in the island of Salsette, which are situated amidst thick and gloomy forests, the growth of many centuries, abounding in wild beasts, and impressing the heart with awe by their trackless solitudes, might have been mistaken by superstitious men for the abodes of demons, especially as the approach to them is by a descent of one or two steps, and the images of the deities sculptured within, besmeared with oil and ochre, have a very fiendlike appearance; but nothing can be more beautiful than the exterior aspect of Ellora. The Bisma Kurm, which forms a portion of the southern extremity of the hill, seems to those whose fancies have been warmed by legends and fairy tales, an appropriate palace for the king of the gnomes, the entrance into subterraneous dominions of singular and unimaginable beauty.

The front of the Bisma Kurm has been rendered perpendicular by cutting away the slope of the hill: it is exceedingly lofty, and its effect is heightened by its receding from the bluff promontory around, and being shadowed by a few trees or shrubs of dark and luxuriant foliage. Over the lower entrance there is an open gallery, which is gained by a

FRONT VIEW OF THE BISMA KURM, CAVES OF ELLORA.

DELHI.

covered stair; and the whole of the decorations are executed with more care than seems to have been taken with the exterior of any of the other caves within the range of the hill. The columns, massy as becomes the weight which they have to support, are richly ornamented, and well proportioned; those of the gallery above are of corresponding dimensions, and the figures in the upper belt are esteemed not inferior in point of execution to any which excite admiration in the neighbouring excavations.

The Bisma Kurm, which Europeans entitle the Carpenter's Cave, is undoubtedly Boodhist; those excavations in the centre of the range alone being entirely Brahminical: the northern caverns are supposed to be devoted to the object of the worship of the Iains; and though the religious opinions of these three sects of Hindoos differ widely from each other, their temples frequently occur in the same district; and in some places, more particularly Ellora, they are united within the same boundary. During the rainy season, when the whole surface of the earth is mantled with grass, and the waterfalls attain a considerable volume, the scenery around the Bisma Kurm is seen to the greatest advantage: the cold weather, however, is better fitted for a visit from European pilgrims; but at no period of the year can these stupendous works be viewed, without exciting the liveliest sensations of delight.

DELHI.

The capital of the Moghul empire, is situated on the left bank of the river Jumna, in lat. 28° 40′ N. and lon. 77° 5′ E. about nine hundred and eighty miles to the north-westward of Calcutta. The subject of the present plate is taken from the modern city, or Shahjehanabad, the designation by which it is distinguished by the natives, who have not yet fallen into the European habit of calling it New Delhi.

In common with all other Indian cities, there is a mixture of meanness and magnificence in every avenue, which conveys melancholy notions of the decay of the place; but, with the exception of the fortunes of the king, which have fallen to a very low ebb, modern Delhi may be said to be in a flourishing condition. Its nobles and merchants are wealthy, and, in a population of nearly 200,000 souls, there is much less of abject poverty than is to be seen in the capitals of independent states. The gateway represented in the engraving affords a beautiful specimen of the Moghul style of architecture. Its tall, graceful minars, with the open lanthorn-like cupola on the top, the massive hall of entrance, battlemented, and crowned with cupolas, appear to great advantage in the wide area partially shaded by trees, which spreads itself in front. Though crowded in some parts, the city of Delhi boasts broader avenues than are usually to be found in Eastern towns, in which the principal thoroughfares are seldom little better than lanes. The Chandry Choke, or Silver Street, leads into the open space which forms the foreground of the plate; it is wide and handsome, and, being shaded by trees and watered by a canal, which runs down the centre, might afford an agreeable promenade, were it not for the native indifference to comfort. Accustomed to live in an atmosphere of flies and dust, the inhabitants of Delhi are not at the trouble of doing any thing to alleviate these nuisances, and strangers, who are anxious to regale themselves with the sights, must make up their minds to be suffocated and smothered. The Chandry Choke always exhibits a lively spectacle; the houses on either side are irregular, some being stuccoed, flat roofed, and of more than one story, the residences of persons of wealth; others are of more crazy materials, looking as if they could not stand against the simooms which occasionally sweep through the city; a line of shabby shops succeeds, then an angle of some more imposing building peeps out, and the whole is intermingled with trees. This street is usually crowded with a very picturesque-looking population. Delhi being a grand mart of commerce, multitudes of persons resort to it from the most distant provinces; rare birds from the hills in cages, cheetahs hooded and led along by their keepers, Persian greyhounds, and Persian cats, are exposed in the streets for sale, the venders sitting or walking perfectly indifferent to the multitudes of hackeries, the strings of camels, the columns of elephants, and the troops of horses which jostle their way through dense throngs of pedestrians, engaged in chaffering, bargaining, quarrelling, or in their various trades which are carried on in the open air outside the houses. Though the sight is both striking and novel, it requires strong nerves to bear the heat, the glare, and the noise. The gaudy colours of the dresses worn by the Moslems and Hindoos, when seen under the beams of a mid-day sun, are exceedingly dazzling; glittering scull-caps, stuck upon one side of the head, are much affected by the Mahommedan dandies, and yellow and pink enter largely into their costume; but if the sight is wearied by gazing upon the vast numbers of shewy figures on horseback, or on foot, mounted upon various animals, or lounging over the balconies and balustraded roofs of the houses, other senses are not less strongly assailed; the noise is absolutely stunning. In addition to men's voices raised to their highest pitch, shouting, hallooing, or talking in all the tongues of Babel; there is the creaking and rumbling of ungreased wheels, the braying of horns, the beating of tomtoms, the neighing of horses, groans of camels, and trumpetings of elephants, mingled with the screams of birds, and the sharp, short roars, or occasional growls, of the hunting leopards: while such a fume arises from the garlic, and other unoderiferous articles employed in the cookery, that the effluvia is almost overpowering. Frequently the confusion is heightened to a tumult by the uproarious progress of the suwarree of some native of rank. The great man sits at his ease on the back of a tall elephant, or lolls lazily in his palanquin, in either case perfectly indifferent to the inconvenience or damage which his retinue may occasion. A promiscuous throng, some on camels, some on horseback, and many on foot, clear the way before him, rushing onward, brandishing their weapons or their maces, and making his titles heard above the din and clamour which would defy less stentorian lungs. Such is a faint picture of the streets of Delhi, which, with their itinerant musicians, their tapestry hangings flowing in long draperies from the tops of the houses, their striped purdahs or curtains, the clinking of makers of hardware, and the glitter of their brass and copper vessels in the sun's rays, must be seen to be duly appreciated.

The walls of the palace are encircled by the open area described in the plate; they enclose a very considerable portion of ground, containing a great variety of buildings more resembling an irregular town than a palace; quadrangle succeeds to quadrangle,

TOMB OF HUMAIOON, — DELHI.

intermixed with ordinary houses, dilapidated stables, and mud huts of the meanest description. Little of the splendour which once surrounded the throne of the Moghul emperors has remained to the unfortunate family who now hold the poor remnant of a once glorious sceptre. The Dewanee Khas, a beautiful open marble pavilion in the hall of audience, still excites the admiration of those who pay their respects to the fallen monarch; but the gems and gold which adorned the peacock throne, and which were estimated at twelve millions of English money, disappeared with Nadir Shah, and, since his visit, the magnificence of the palace has dwindled yearly. Adjoining the palace, and connected with it by a bridge, is a fortress-like building of dark red granite, built in the sixteenth century, under Selim, and named after him Selimgurgh, which for many years served as a prison to those who had incurred the royal displeasure. The largest of the towers, called Shah-boorg, royal tower, is particularly attractive to an English eye, in consequence of a picturesque incident attached to it. Mirza Irwann Buckt, heir apparent to the throne, made his escape from it in 1784, being let down from one of its windows by the turbans of his followers, unrolled and made into a ladder; reaching the ground in safety, he sought protection from the British government.

The English language has made greater progress at Delhi than in any other city of the upper provinces of India; it is no uncommon circumstance for strangers in the European dress, in quest of lions, to be greeted by respectable-looking inhabitants in their own tongue. "Good morning," or "How do you do, sir?" are the usual salutations; these persons have received their education in the English college established in the city, an institution which is likely to attract a greater share of government patronage than it has hitherto enjoyed. To the intelligence and good conduct of one of its students, Lieutenant Burnes has borne honourable testimony, in the well-merited praise which he has bestowed upon Mohunlàl, the faithful companion of his travels.

English equipages and English furniture are in a good deal of request amongst the natives; the horse and buggy are seen to supplant the bullock and rhut, and even the elephant, formerly the conveyances of men of moderate fortune. Prince Baber, the king's second son, appears in public in an English chariot drawn by eight horses, and is fond of substituting the uniform coat of a general officer for the Hindoostanee upper vestment; this, however, he chooses to adorn with two grand crosses of the Bell, one on each breast. Prince Mirza, a younger brother, also drives an English carriage, and the names and callings of many of the shopkeepers are blazoned over the doors in English characters, while the shops themselves are filled with all sorts of European manufactures.

HUMAIOON'S TOMB.

The mausoleum of a prince, not more celebrated for his misfortunes than his virtues, forms one of the most perfect edifices which are still to be found amid the ruins of old Delhi. The tomb of Humaioon is situated at about five miles distance from the southern or Agra gate; it is a noble pile of granite, inlaid with white marble, less florid and of a simpler style of architecture than that of his more celebrated son at Secundra. The basement is a terrace two hundred feet square, raised upon cloisters, and having a wide flight of steps on each side; the central building is also square, containing one large circular hall, with smaller apartments at the angles, the whole being crowned with a marble dome, and the pediments of four handsome gateways. According to the Asiatic custom the body of the emperor is interred in a sepulchre upon the basement floor. The sarcophagus, which is small, of white marble, raised at a small elevation from the pavement, is placed immediately over the body in the centre of the circular hall before mentioned. The interior exhibits the remains of rich decorations of gilding and enamel, and tassels of gold formerly depended from the roof; these, however, became a prey to the devastating propensities of the Jauts, who amused themselves by firing their matchlocks at them, the marks of the bullets are distinctly to be traced in the dome and other parts of this superb edifice. Several members belonging to Humaioon's family lie entombed beneath the chambers at the angles, having sarcophagi on the upper floor; these are beautifully carved in white marble, and the whole is simple, chaste, and of a noble plainness.

The mausoleum stood in the centre of a large garden, surrounded by a battlemented wall, cloistered on the inside, flanked by towers, and having four gateways. This garden, with its stately groves, its terraces, and fountains, is now a wilderness; by the aid of the only spring of water, which has not dried up, some poor families, who live in the outbuildings of the tomb, cultivate a little grain for their subsistence, but sand has encroached upon the pastures; and, from the terrace above, the view is over desolated plains, covered with ruins, and bounded by a range of hills equally bleak and barren.

The tomb of Humaioon is seen to the left of the plate, with all that is still entire of its surrounding walls: the fore-ground affords a faithful portraiture of the rugged soil, cumbered with fragments of temples, towers, and palaces, which now marks the site of old Delhi. In the distance to the right, gateways and other dome-crowned tombs appear, intermingled with a scanty foliage of shrubs, one solitary palm rearing its head over the prostrate ruins.

The history of Humaioon is full of romantic and chivalric incident. In the early part of his life he became the sworn knight of one of the princesses of Rajasthan, who, according to the custom of her country, secured the sword of the prince in her service by the gift of a bracelet. The *Rakhi bund Bhae*, or bracelet bound brother, feels himself called upon to espouse the cause of the lady from whom he has received the gift, and to defend her against all her enemies whenever she shall demand his assistance. The princess Kurnivati, closely besieged at Cheetore, sent to Humaioon, then prosecuting a vigorous campaign in Bengal, he instantly obeyed the summons, and, though too late to save, evinced his fidelity by avenging the fall of the city. Kurnivati, at the head of thirteen thousand females, had shut herself up in a cavern filled with combustible materials, and perished rather than submit to the conqueror; the flower of Rajasthan had fallen in the defence of Cheetore, and Humaioon only came in time to wrest the sword from the victor, whom he defeated in a battle fought without the walls. The affairs of his own kingdom soon occupied all his attention; he was engaged in numerous wars, with ambitious aspirants to the throne, and, after many vicissitudes of fortune, the star of Shere Khan prevailed, and he was driven to seek a refuge in Persia. It is said, that as the Orientals scrupulously observe the flights of birds, and imagine that the fortunes of men may be deduced from them, the attendants of the fugitive prince drew a favourable augury from the appearance of an eagle, which, when Homaioon, fatigued with his journey, had flung himself on the bare earth to snatch a short repose, hovered over his head, affording a shelter from the sun by its extended wings. This was esteemed a happy omen, and his companions predicted that he would be restored to his kingdom, and reign over it with greater glory than before.

Upon his arrival in Persia, the ease and courtesy of Humaioon's manners, the manliness of his spirit, and the ready grace with which he extricated himself from embarrassing situations, secured him many friends. He was received in the first interview with the monarch, to whom he had fled, in a garden. Either by accident or design, the only seat which happened to be upon the spot was not large enough to accommodate more than one person. Perplexed and mortified by an incident which might oblige him to acknowledge his inferiority, Humaioon paused for a moment, but instantly recovering his presence of mind, he invited the Persian prince to sit, and placing himself on the left hand, which is the post of honour in the east, formed a seat by resting his bow against the sopha, thus avoiding the disgrace of standing in the presence of the king, whose aid he came to implore. The Persian monarch, it is said, was struck by the dignity of mind which the fugitive displayed in this incident, and treated him in a manner becoming his rank. Humaioon, we are told, was greatly indebted both to the hospitality of the king of Persia, and the aid which he afforded him in the recovery of his throne, he returned the obligation by giving great encouragement to the Kuzzilbashes, whose favour at court inclined many to suppose that he belonged to the Sheeah sect of Mahommedans. Ferishta, however, asserts that he was a Soonnee of the Hunesy persuasion, though there are great doubts whether he could be considered very orthodox by true believers. After his return from exile, Humaioon, contrary to the former policy displayed by the Moghul emperors, attached himself to the Rajpoots, promoting many to high offices. It is said that he carried his complaisance so far as to mingle with these idolaters in their temples, and assist at their ceremonies, acts which, as it may be supposed, brought great scandal upon his religious principles, and even laid him under the imputation of worshipping the sun.

Different accounts are given of the mode of his death, which took place in 1556, within a year after his final restoration to the throne: according to some writers, he fell from the walls of his own tomb, the rod with which he was measuring the different portions breaking as he leaned upon it, and precipitating him to the foundation; but Ferishta, who is the better authority of the two, gives another version of the story. He tells us that while Humaioon was in the act of descending the steps leading from a terrace, the Muezzin announced the hour of prayer. The king, according to custom, stood still, and repeated the creed of Islam, sitting down at its conclusion on the second step, until the criers had ended. When about to rise, he assisted himself with a staff, which slipping along the marble pavement, his body was overbalanced and fell headlong to the ground. He was taken up insensible, and, after languishing a few days, rendered up his spirit to his Creator.

Humaioon is described to have been handsome in his person, and finely formed, mild and benevolent almost to a fault, since his enemies took advantage of the clemency of his disposition. He was highly accomplished, according to the notions of his day, taking great delight in the study of astronomy and geography, and in the society of learned men; specimens of his compositions are extant, which prove him to be no mean poet, but he was unfortunately addicted to the use of opium, and the fine qualities of his mind were sometimes obscured by the effects of this debasing habit. He died at the age of fifty-one, and is indebted to his son Akbar for the beautiful mausoleum which rises above his ashes.

CAWNPORE.

The native city of Cawnpore extends along the Ganges on the western side, in the province of Allahabad, about 650 miles from Calcutta. Though many persons have looked for the site of Palibrotha at this place, they have been completely unsuccessful, not a single vestige of a city of such great celebrity being to be found. Cawnpore, though having, like all other oriental towns, a pretty appearance from the river, is meanly built, and boasts of no edifice of particular note. It, however, presents several interesting landscapes: isolated mosques, or pagodas, surrounded by a few trees, being of constant recurrence. Two of these temples appear in the plate, built according to the old Hindoo custom, not now invariably followed, with mitred shaped domes; the white building to the left is the house of a wealthy native, and two bungalows in the occupation of British officers are seen in the distant perspective.

The view of the city on the land side is a good deal shut out by a wooded ridge, skirting a sandy plain, which divides it from the cantonments. When the setting sun lights up the towers and pinnacles, which peep between the rich foliage of the trees, the gazer is apt to form an erroneous judgment of the picturesqueness and splendour of the interior: there is absolutely nothing to repay the perambulator for the dust which he must encounter in a nearer survey.

Cawnpore is a very important military station, it faces the king of Oude's territories on the opposite bank of the river, and is always garrisoned by an imposing force. The cantonments, which are very irregular and scattered over a large surface of ground, are at least five miles in length. They present a very agreeable succession of houses, gardens, and park-like grounds; these have been literally reclaimed from the desert, for although Cawnpore is situated in the Doaab, which is celebrated for its richness and fertility, the country immediately around it is one wide waste of sand. Quitting the cantonments we find the houses of the civilians at Nawaub-gunge, in the midst of desolation, and at the other extremity, the same characteristics prevail, the encamping ground occupied by the troops in the cold season being absolutely treeless and leafless, and frequently presenting the phenomena of the Mirage. The cantonments are a good deal diversified by ravines, and being thickly planted and interspersed by native temples and village-like bazaars,

CAWNPORE.

JUMMA MUSJID.—MANDOO.

afford a great variety of interesting drives. The houses, though principally bungalows, are upon a very large scale, and their general appearance is much improved by the addition of bowed ends, stuccoed with chunam, and bearing a resemblance to stone edifices. Many of these bungalows boast very splendid suites of apartments, and are fitted up in the interior in a manner which does infinite credit to the native workmen employed. All are furnished with one or more fire places, the severity of the weather in the cold season rendering a blazing hearth essential to comfort. The gardens are in a high state of cultivation, and are exceedingly productive. All the European vegetables, with the exception of broad or Windsor beans, come to great perfection in the cold season, and, in addition to those of native growth, the nole-cole, an importation from the Cape, is in much esteem. Citrons, shaddocks, oranges, sweet lemons, and limes, are abundant, the trees being literally loaded with their golden fruitage: the mango, plantain, guava, and custard apple, are equally plentiful, together with melons in the season, and the finest peaches and grapes which Hindoostan can produce. The bazaars are well supplied with butcher's meat, poultry, and game, the river furnishes many kinds of fish, and there are English farmers, or provisioners, as they are called, settled in the cantonments, who feed pigs, and cure excellent bacon and hams. The assembly rooms and the theatre are two very fine buildings, particularly the latter, which is surrounded by a corridor supported by pillars of the Ionic order; there is unfortunately no church, the service being performed alternately in the riding-house belonging to the king's dragoons, and a bungalow fitted up for the purpose at the other end of the cantonments. Engineer officers have declined to undertake the work for the sum offered by government, and the residents refuse to subscribe to make up the surplus required, in consequence of the apprehension of further curtailments, should it appear that they had any money to spare. A fine avenue of trees, which is selected for the evening drive, leads to the race-course, the roads are well watered, and the hog and tiger hunting in the neighbourhood, though not equal to that in wilder tracts of the country, is sufficient to afford good sport to the enterprizing.

There is a great deal of military duty to be done at Cawnpore, and it is consequently not a favourite station; there are also many temptations to expense, which are not held out in smaller communities; but these drawbacks are more than compensated by the choice of society, the facility of procuring European articles, especially books, and the constant intercourse with persons proceeding up and down the country, all affording a most agreeable variety to the usual monotony of a Mofussil station.

JUMMA MUSJID—MANDOO.

Those only who have had an opportunity of remarking the noble countenances, exalted stature, and dignified bearing of the few specimens of the tribe, who, in the humble capacity of apple merchants and camel drivers, make annual visits to Hindoostan, can form an adequate notion of the splendid natural gifts lavished on the Afghans. They claim to be of Jewish origin, and, though their features resembling portraits of the Jews by the old masters, their names, and many of their customs, favour the belief, but the proofs are incomplete. The Afghans owed their first introduction into Hindoostan to the commercial dealings which they carried on between that country and Persia; but, establishing themselves upon the throne of Delhi, they became for a time masters of the kingdom, and have left in many parts numerous memorials of their former supremacy. The Jumma Musjid at Mandoo is said to be the finest and largest specimen of the Afghan mosque at present to be found in India. Its wild and desolate aspect, as it appears in the accompanying plate, is exactly correspondent with the state of the city, deserted and reduced to a heap of ruins. Mandoo has already been described as the ancient capital of the Dhar Rajahs; standing on the summit of one of the mountains of the Vhyndian range; it was formerly a place of considerable importance—strong by nature, and rendered still more so by art; but, since its reduction by Akbar, it has fallen into decay, being, for a long time prior to the British conquests in Malwa, a stronghold of Bheel robbers. The remains of a part of the piazza, declare that the Jumma Musjid at Mandoo was formerly enclosed in a quadrangle, according to the usual style of similar edifices in India; the smallness and roundness of the cupola shew the peculiar characteristics of Afghan architecture; domes of similar construction are to be seen in the ruins of the adjoining college, now nearly reduced to a heap of stones. The small number of human beings who now share the city with numerous families of wild beasts, consist of a few Hindoo devotees, who are at little pains to defend themselves from the attacks of tigers, conceiving that death from one of these animals affords a sure passport to heaven.

There is scarcely any mention whatsoever of Mandoo in a journey from Agra to Oojein, a city only sixty-five miles distant, performed in 1792, though the travellers crossed the Chumbul not far from its source, near the mountain city. The buildings of Mandoo are chiefly built of red schistus, which is found in the neighbourhood; and the scenery is described as being very beautiful, especially on the banks of the Chumbul, which presents a large body of rapidly-running water, bounded by hills of different elevations, and the most picturesque forms. The water of the Chumbul is extremely clear, and it is overshadowed in many places by groves of trees. The fertility of the soil, and the favourable nature of the climate, are exemplified by the redundance of vegetation which has sprung up in every part of Mandoo; trees have planted their roots amid the stone-work of the Jumma Musjid, and its once paved area is overgrown with shrubby plants and long jungle grass, now the haunt of tigers, which lodge in its palaces, and bring forth their young in the halls of kings.

There is little chance that Malwa will become sufficiently flourishing and populous to fill Mandoo with inhabitants, before its neglected buildings shall have fallen into utter and irremediable decay. New generations will probably choose new sites for their cities, and, in a short time, the last vestiges of its former glory will have wholly disappeared.

VIEWS IN

I N D I A.

C H I N A,

AND ON

THE SHORES OF THE RED SEA;

DRAWN BY

PROUT, STANFIELD, CATTERMOLE, PURSER, COX, AUSTEN, &c.

FROM ORIGINAL SKETCHES

BY

COMMANDER ROBERT ELLIOTT, R. N.

WITH

DESCRIPTIONS BY EMMA ROBERTS.

VOL. II.

ADDRESS.

In completing the Second Volume of their work, the Proprietors feel anxious to address a few words to their Subscribers, trusting that their efforts to procure the most original and authentic accounts of the scenes and places represented in the various Engravings which have embellished the preceding pages, will ensure for them the continuance of public favour, which they have felt to be so flattering and so honourable.

It is not without a just feeling ot pride that the Proprietors of Fisher's Views state, that to their active and strenuous endeavours the European world have been indebted for a more extensive acquaintance with the British possessions in India, than has ever before been presented to the public in so comprehensive and so cheap a form. The descriptions of the manners, habits, feelings, governments, and policy of the natives of India, have been as copious as the limits of the design would admit; and those who have not had an opportunity of consulting other works upon the subject, may form an accurate idea of the principal features of the most interesting portions of Asia, from the illustrations, literary and pictorial, which are comprised in the present volumes.

In taking leave of their Subscribers for the present, the Proprietors beg to state, that having made large purchases of finished Sketches, taken on the spot, it is their intention to commence a New Series of their work in the course of a few months, in which they will have the honour to introduce a considerable number of Views of various parts of the Himalaya.

It is scarcely necessary to dilate upon the very interesting nature of the scenery of a part of the world which is now attracting almost universal attention. The sublimity of the prospects of the Himalaya, its magnificent forests, its eternal snows, romantic passes, and flashing rivers, have burst upon the eyes of Europe with all the freshness of a newly-discovered country; and the greatest anxiety is manifested to obtain a more accurate knowledge of a region so rich in all the productions of nature, and which offers so fair a field for philosophic investigation. There is every reason to suppose that the Himalaya mountains will, by affording a climate suited to European constitutions, become the principal residence of those colonists who are desirous of carrying British capital and British science into India. Under these circumstances, the proprietors are convinced that they cannot offer a more acceptable work to the public, than that which opens so bright a prospect of the continuance and prosperity of our empire in the East, and which is in itself so fruitful in all that can afford interest to those who love to contemplate Nature in all her varied forms.

The Drawings will be by Allom, Bentley, Daniell, Dibden, Melville, Purser, Stanfield, Turner, &c.

CONTENTS OF VOL. II.

TOMB OF SHERE SHAH.

ILLUSTRATIONS

OF

INDIA,

CHINA, AND THE SHORES OF THE RED SEA.

SHERE SHAH'S TOMB AT SASSERAM.

THE town of Sasseram is situated in the district of Shahabad, which forms a portion of the picturesque and fertile province of Behar; it is about thirty-four miles to the south of Buxar, and the new road from Calcutta to Benares runs directly through it. Strangers travelling through the Bengal presidency do not, until after they have passed the city of Patna, come upon any of those wonders of Moslem architecture for which northern India is so justly celebrated.

The majestic solemnity and sober plainness of the dark grey pile which rears its dome-crowned roof over the remains of the most remarkable personage of his day, are indicative of the antiquity of the building, for at this period marble had not entered into the composition of the imperial edifices of Hindostan. This splendid material was sparingly used in the time of Humaioon. Akbar employed it with a more lavish hand; but it was not until the reign of Shah Jehan that it was piled in the rich profusion which excites so much delighted surprise in the scenes where that tasteful monarch reigned and revelled. The tomb of Shere rises in the centre of an immense reservoir of water, three or four hundred yards square. This tomb is surrounded by a high embankment, constructed of the earth which was dug out of its foundation, and along each side there runs a flight of stone steps, affording access to the water from every part. The tomb is raised upon a square platform in the centre of a terrace, approached from the water by handsome flights of steps; and it was formerly connected with the main land by a bridge of five arches, the remains of which appear in the accompanying engraving. The angles of the platform are flanked by low cupola'd towers, and there is a small but very handsome arched gateway leading to the bridge.

The tomb itself is octagonal, and consists of two stories beneath the dome, each having a flat terrace running round it, adorned with small pavilion-like turrets, open at the sides, and cupola'd at the top. The summit of the dome was originally crowned with one of these cupolas, supported upon four slender pillars, and adding an air of grace and elegance to the massive edifice below. The tomb is constructed of stone furnished from the neighbouring hills, and very neatly joined together, though destitute of the carved work which gives so florid an appearance to the elaborately ornamented mausoleums of Agra and Delhi. The small cupola'd turrets have a coating of stucco, intended in all probability to receive those blue enamelled tiles which are seen in the decorations of buildings of this period, and with which similar cupolas springing round the tomb of Akbar are covered. The interior is equally plain, containing several sarcophagi, in which the enterprising Afghan and his family lie enshrined.

In the absence of bridge or boat, the natives have a curious method of ferrying themselves across the tank to Shere Shah's tomb; they insert the four legs of a charpoy, or bedstead, into earthen vessels called kedgeree pots, which float the raft, and, seating themselves upon it, they paddle over, taking care, of course, not to strike the jars, as a single fracture would send them at once to the bottom. The redundance of foliage now springing through the interstices which time has made in the basement story of Shere Shah's tomb, affords melancholy indications of its approaching demolition. Should these shrubs be permitted to remain, the rapidity of their growth will soon undermine the foundation, and in a very short time the ruins of this splendid building will choke up the surrounding tank.

Shere Shah, like many other Moslem princes, did not leave the care of his ashes to posterity, but constructed his mausoleum during the flourishing period of his reign. He inherited the district of Sasseram from his father Hussein, who had received it as the reward of his services to the subahdah of Jaunpore. He distinguished himself at a very early period of life, and his original appellation of Ferid was soon lost in the more popular title bestowed upon him in consequence of an exploit with a tiger, which he killed by a single stroke of his sabre, while at a hunting party with Mahmood, who had raised himself to the sovereignty of Behar. From this time he was known by the name of Shere Khan: Shere signifies lion, a title frequently given to the slayers of those savage beasts, and which was subsequently won by the brave and unfortunate Afkun, the first husband of Nour Mahal.

Shere Khan was an Afghan by descent, of the Ghorian family, and it is said, that in a visit to the Moghul camp in the days of Baber, he conceived the design of wresting the empire from the descendants of Tamerlane, and restoring it to the race of its earlier sovereigns. Prosecuting this design through various vicissitudes of fortune, during fifteen years of unremitting warfare, he at length achieved his object, and, driving the unfortunate Humaioon into exile, seated himself upon the throne of Delhi. Had Shere Khan succeeded to the empire of Hindostan by descent, he would doubtless have won the affection of his contemporaries, and the admiration of posterity: but the nobler qualities of his mind were obscured by ambition; he thirsted for power, and obtained a throne at the expense of many crimes, staining the royal dignity by acts of treachery, necessary perhaps to secure the position in which he had placed himself, but unjustifiable in themselves, and odious in the eyes of the people.

Though little scrupulous in his private conduct, and reckless of the means which promised to maintain his sovreignty, Shere Shah was not unmindful of the public weal,

SARNÂT, A BOODH MONUMENT NEAR BENARES.

and endeavoured, by the establishment of many useful institutions, to reconcile the people of India to his usurpation. He encouraged commerce, by affording merchants from distant countries facilities for travelling, and for the transportation of their goods, by making roads, and building caravanserais after the model of those which existed in Persia. From Bengal and Saunargaum to the Nilâb, a branch of the Indus, at the distance of three thousand English miles, he dug a well at the end of every two miles, planted the road with fruit trees, and secured accommodation for men and cattle at each stage of the journey. A certain number of domestics were maintained at these serais, and the charges were regulated by law. He introduced convenient weights and measures and established horse-posts for the conveyance of intelligence to government, which were also available to private individuals, as the medium of correspondence with remote districts, which had hitherto been attended with great difficulties, and had proved a serious hinderance to commercial speculations.

The death of Shere is variously related: by some writers it is averred, that, being a very expert marksman and fond of fire-arms, he made an essay with his own hands, of the capacity of a large piece of ordnance sent to him from Bengal: the gun being too heavily charged, burst when the match was applied, and a fragment striking the emperor killed him on the spot. Ferishta attributes the catastrophe to a different cause, and tells us, that Shere's death was occasioned by the bursting of a shell, which blew up a powder magazine of a battery in which he stood while laying siege to Kallinger, one of the formidable hill fortresses of Bundelkhund, and supposed to be the strongest place of defence in Hindostan. The warlike monarch, though desperately wounded, allowed not his spirit to share in his bodily sufferings, but still continued to cheer on his troops to the attack. The place was vigorously assaulted, and in the evening the soldier's dying moments were soothed by intelligence of its reduction. Exclaiming, "Thanks to Almighty God," he breathed his last.

SARNAT—A BOODH MONUMENT NEAR BENARES.

Few things have been productive of more doubt and perplexity to the learned world, than the remains of the round towers, all apparently springing from one common origin, which are found in different and remote parts of the globe. The extraordinary monument, of which a representation is given in the accompanying plate, is undoubtedly Boodhist: it stands near the European station of Secrole, about four miles distant from the city of Benares, and it is an object of great curiosity and interest to all antiquarian travellers. This tower is about a hundred and fifty feet in circumference, and its remains are above a hundred feet in height; it is very solidly constructed, the lower part having a casing of large blocks of stone neatly joined together, well polished, and decorated near the base with a broad belt carved with flowers.

By some persons it is supposed that the upper portion is the addition of a later period; it is built of brick, the casing of stone (if it ever existed) has disappeared altogether, and the ruinous state of the summit affords no clue to its original conformation. It is, however, imagined to have been of a pyramidal or globular shape, the forms of these holy places being generally similar to the gigantic mounds which in ancient times were raised over the ashes of the dead. In fact, the temples of the Boodhists are usually tombs, or buildings which commemorate the actions of men. There is no all-pervading influence in their deity, who is supposed to maintain a quiescent state, untroubled by the government of the world, and wholly unconcerned about the affairs of men. The followers of Boodh imagine, that although their god takes very little interest in the good or evil actions of his creatures, which are rewarded and punished in this world, prosperity being the universal consequence of virtue, and misfortune the constant attendant upon vice; that sanctity of a very superior order, extraordinary acts of self-denial, and the good wrought by the reformation of their brethren, secures to the devotee rigidly performing these and other duties, the power of working miracles, and even after death a certain degree of those god-like attributes which may be employed to influence the destinies of mankind. The religious worship of the Boodhists is paid to these saints and prophets, and the time-defying towers affording such conclusive proof of the wide dissemination of their doctrines, which are found in opposite quarters of the globe, are said to contain either the bodies, or some relic, a tooth, or the hair, of these holy persons.

It is a very extraordinary fact, that although the Boodhist and the Brahminical religions are strongly opposed to each other, the followers of the latter believing Boodh to be an avatar of Vishnu, incarnated for the purpose of leading mankind into error, and only admitting him into their temples under that character, that the sacred edifices of the two hostile sects are found in juxta-position with each other, as at Ellora and Elephanta; and that there is a pagoda in the close vicinity of Sarnat, which is esteemed by the Brahmins to stand upon ground more highly blessed than any other in the neighbourhood of the holy city of Benares.

The foundations of a very large building are to be traced at about the distance of two hundred yards from the tower, and it is supposed that at this place the priests belonging to the adjacent temple had a religious establishment, it being their custom to assemble in bodies in the neighbourhood of the temple dedicated to the objects of their religious worship. These remains, some forty or fifty years ago, attracted the attention of several scientific gentlemen, at that time residents in the European cantonments of Seerole, and they commenced an active research by digging in many places around. Their labours were rewarded by the discovery of several excavations filled with an immense number of flat tiles, having representations of Boodh modelled upon them in wax. It is said by the writer's authority, a gentleman to whose taste and talents the European world is indebted for information relative to India of the most interesting nature, that there were actually cart-loads of these images found in the excavations before mentioned; many were deposited in the museums and collections of private individuals, but whether they were ever made the subject of a descriptive account seems doubtful, there being at least no public document of the kind.

The silver and marble images, now so constantly seen in the curiosity shops of London, seated, with hands folded over their knees, composed features, and attitudes of deep repose, have familiarized a great number of persons with the objects of Boodhist worship.

TRIAD FIGURE, INTERIOR OF ELEPHANTA.

Though the posture is somewhat varied by the figure being represented standing, it is always calm and meditative, and, being the semblances of men, these images are invariably shaped in strict accordance with the human form. There are none of the fantastic devices intended to convey ideas of the superior bodily and intellectual powers of the gods which have created the monstrosities of the Hindoo pantheon; no triple-headed or quadruple-armed chimeras, with the feet of beasts and the wings of griffins, with which the Brahminical temples are so profusely decorated.

There cannot be any religion so unimaginative as that of the Boodhists; their notions of eternal bliss are confined to the absence of all care and pain; they have figured to themselves a supreme being slumbering over the busy world; and even the sources of good and evil; virtue and vice have not inspired their sluggish souls with those lively images which naturally arise in the mind at the contemplation of their effect upon the happiness of man.

There is a Boodhist temple at Gya, a place also remarkable for being a favourite seat of the religious worship of the Brahmins; it is in better preservation, and more highly ornamented, than the monument of Sarnat, of which, however, the carved work has considerable claims to notice. The figure of Boodh appears upon a peculiar kind of medallion richly enwreathed with leaves and flowers, and there are the remains of eight projections, each having a niche in the centre, and each protruding about eight inches beyond the solid mass; three of them are shewn in the engraving, but the ornaments of the remainder of this remarkable structure, if it possessed any, have been swept away by the remorseless hand of time.

TRIAD FIGURE—INTERIOR OF ELEPHANTA.

The colossal three-headed bust, which fronts the entrance of the principal excavation of Elephanta, is the most attractive, as well as the most striking object to be found amidst the rich sculptures of the subterranean cathedral represented in the accompanying plate. It occupies a conspicuous situation at the extreme end of the cavern, and has occasioned much conjectures and many controversies; some writers supposing it to be a representation of the three personages which are said to constitute the Hindoo trinity, although it is by no means certain that Brahma, Vishnu, and Siva have ever been associated in this manner; while others have pronounced it to be three of the forms under which the last-mentioned deity is worshipped.

The three-headed figure at Elephanta is of gigantic dimensions, measuring seventeen feet ten inches from the top of the cap of the central head to the termination at the breast; that which fronts the spectator is full-faced, those to the right and left are in profile; and by some it is asserted that Siva, whose impersonations are frequently surrounded by almost innumerable characteristic attributes, had, or was intended to have, a fourth head corresponding with that in front, and that, therefore, only half of the group is given in the sculptures of Elephanta. The whole of this singular triad is hewn out of the solid rock, which is a coarse-grained dark grey basaltic formation, called by the geologists trachyte; it lies in a recess cut into the rock to the depth of thirteen feet, including the thickness of the door-way, screen, or wall, projecting beyond it, which is about two feet and a half. The basement is raised about two feet nine inches from the ground; at each corner of the threshold are holes apparently for the purpose of receiving door-posts, and a groove runs along the floor in front, which it is imagined was intended to receive a screen, let down occasionally to conceal the group.

Though there are numerous opinions upon the subject, the most learned personages seem to agree that this vast temple was dedicated solely to Siva, who is here represented with only three of the five heads with which he is frequently delineated. The workmanship exhibits considerable skill and beauty, although the art was evidently in its infancy at the period of its execution. Dimly seen through the long perspective of the pillared aisle, it is wonderfully imposing, and, upon a nearer approach, the details afford an equal degree of surprise and delight. The cap of the eastern head is richly adorned with variegated figures of flowers and branches, intermingled with symbols which are peculiar to Siva, and by which he is always distinguished, each Hindoo deity being recognised by his emblematic devices. The principal head is too much defaced to be so confidently pronounced to belong to the greatest of the gods, and hence the difficulties which have arisen in deciding whether Siva is alone entitled to the honours of this magnificent triad, or if he must share them with Brahma and Vishnu.

The great temple at Elephanta is nearly square, being a hundred and thirty feet deep, and about a hundred and thirty-three feet broad; it is divided into nine aisles formed of twenty-six pillars, of which eight are broken, and some of the remainder much injured: there are several recesses somewhat similar to the chapels attached to the cathedrals of Europe, scooped out at the sides, and these, together with the adjacent walls, are covered with sculptures. Time has been busily at work with these curious effigies, and its ravages unfortunately have been aided by the superstitious fanaticism of the Portuguese, whose religious zeal incited them to the destruction of every relic of idolatry, however curious and wonderful as a work of art, on which they might venture to display their indignation. It is said that they went a very ingenious way to work to effect their object at Elephanta, by lighting large fires in different parts of the cave: after the pillars had become intensely heated, they threw cold water upon them, which, by causing sudden expansion, occasioned the stone to split in all directions. Some of the pillars, the capitals of which are seen in the accompanying plate, have evidently been subjected to this destructive process; others, though still standing, are much injured, large splinters being taken off from the top to the bottom, while very few of the figures have escaped mutilation.

We are told, that a Portuguese gentleman of high rank, in the fervour of his religious enthusiasm, was wont to employ himself by firing at the offending sculptures with a great gun. Determined geologists have effected nearly as much mischief, by their devastating hammers: striking off toes and fingers in the most merciless manner, for the sake of obtaining specimens; a less excusable act of wantonness than that recorded of the Portuguese worthy, since he offended through ignorance, while these perpetrations were the result of a pretended love of science.

MOSQUE OF MUSTAPHA KHAN,—BEEJAPORE.

The decay but too visible at Elephanta, is farther accelerated by pools of water formed during the periodical inundations, and which sap away the bases of the pillars. From the extraordinary damage effected in the course of a few years by this cause, Bishop Heber has, perhaps too hastily, decided, that these wonderful excavations are comparatively modern. Like the caves of Ellora, the period of their formation is involved in the most impenetrable doubt and obscurity, the traditions are so vague and unsatisfactory as to afford no assistance in arriving at any probable conclusion. Temples dedicated to gods, still the cherished objects of Hindoo worship, have been desecrated from time immemorial, the surrounding followers of Brahma only surveying the sculptured effigies of their most highly esteemed gods on the walls of these splendid excavations, with the same respect which they paid the images resembling them, which the Sepoys of Sir David Baird's army found, to their great astonishment, in Egypt. The occurrence of these caves in one peculiar portion of the peninsula, and upon ground exclusively occupied by the Mahrattas, render the supposition that they were the work of some great people, insulated from the rest of the world, and whose existence has been forgotten in the lapse of ages, very probable. This empire must have lasted many years, to produce works requiring such extraordinary and persevering labour, and it must also have been characterized by the most liberal notions on the subject of religious tolerance, since it has admitted temples belonging to sects violently opposed to each other, into close and apparently amicable neighbourhood.

MOSQUE OF MUSTAPHA KHAN, BEEJAPORE.

Former visitants to the city of Beejapore, while expressing their admiration at the varied and beautiful architectural remains still to be found in the highest preservation amid a wild waste of ruins, have pointed them out as well worthy the attention of scientific persons, whose previous studies and cultivated taste would render them better adapted to the task of description than military men, who may be said merely to act the part of pioneers, leading the way for the more learned and efficient traveller. Hitherto, however, the slight notices scattered through several highly-esteemed works upon India, have not attracted the attention of those who could alone do justice to the multitudinous objects of interest with which this extraordinary city abounds. Beejapore has only been the casual sojourn of a few idlers and amateurs, who have contented themselves, or have been compelled for want of time to be content, with a very hasty and cursory glance; the most diligent have left the greater part of the splendours springing up on every side wholly undescribed, and, amidst many others, we vainly seek for any detailed account of the mosque of Mustapha Khan.

This beautiful edifice stands near the centre of the city, in an open area leading from the principal street. The surrounding quadrangle is entered by a large massive gateway, under a noble arch. Time, which has been busy with the buildings which lie prostrate and in ruins on every side, seems to have almost wholly spared the mosque which rears its dark walls nearly uninjured in the midst of utter desolation. This temple, though far inferior in size to the Jumma Musjid, is lofty and beautifully proportioned; and the external ornaments, though of a less florid character than those of many other structures in its neighbourhood, are chaste and appropriate, while there is something peculiarly elegant in the shape and decorations of the dome. The high narrow arches which run along the front, and are continued throughout the interior, afford a variety to the ordinary style, and the effect of their perspective is exceedingly pleasing. To this meagre account of a building which merits a much more elaborate description, nothing at present can be added, but we may hope that the general cultivation of taste for works of art, and the unexpected facilities of visiting a city, which at no distant period belonged to an enemy's country, and was almost inaccessible to European footsteps, will greatly increase our information respecting so interesting a place as Beejapore.

There are various traditions and legends attached to this romantic capital, which still live in the recollection of its few inhabitants; and travellers acquainted with the language as they survey with rapt delight the gorgeous remains of a once flourishing kingdom, are entertained by the tales and explanations of their native conductors.

A small pool of water is pointed out to the curious, which possesses a high degree of sanctity in the eyes of the Hindoos, and which the Moslems, who believe in many of their neighbour's marvels, look upon with great respect. It is milky in its appearance, but perfectly wholesome, no other spring of the same kind is to be found in any part of the neighbourhood, and none presume to doubt the truth of the tradition which ascribes it to the piety of a Brahmin, who brought a small quantity of the holy water of the Ganges to this remote spot. Rapidly increasing into the pool which is still in existence, it maintains its distinct character, and affords to all devout persons a proof of the miraculous nature of the sacred river.

A still more intesting story is told about a tomb, named, in consequence of the pure whiteness and brilliant lustre of the stucco with which it is lined, Mootee Gil,—mootee signifying pearl. A nobleman who had amassed an enormous quantity of wealth, had the misfortune to awaken the avaricious propensities of his sovereign, who felt an eager desire to transfer the coveted treasures to his own coffers, and scrupled not to employ means in common use among Eastern despots. It was determined to bring an accusation of treason against him, and, under this plea, to seize upon and sequestrate his riches. The plot was deeply and cunningly laid, but its intended victim having obtained timely information of his danger, explained to the ladies of his family the predicament in which he stood, and consulted with them upon the best means of avoiding its most fatal consequences.

It happened that the greater part of the nobleman's envied acquisitions consisted of pearls and other ornaments for the Zenana. The faithful and devoted females, whom he apprised of his danger, immediately devised a plan, which, though it involved the sacrifice of objects dear to woman's vanity, promised to secure a still dearer life. They proposed to break the pearls, which had excited the king's cupidity, into pieces, and they were accordingly nearly reduced to powder. The destruction of these gems becoming a topic of public notoriety, it was no longer worth while to molest the owner, who, though impoverished, spent the residue of his days in tranquillity.

KING'S FORT,— BOORHANPORE.

The broken pearls remained a long time in the family, but at length came into the possession of a faqueer named Maloone Hulbec Allah, who employed them in the decoration of a mausoleum, which he built for himself. Reduced to an impalpable powder, and formed, according to the ordinary process used with marble dust, into chunam, he coated the whole of the interior with this precious material, which retains all the delicate hue and shining qualities of the pearls of which it is said to be composed.

Travellers who have related this tale, while declaring that it is impossible for them to attest its truth, also state, that the splendour of the stucco affords strong reason for the supposition, that something more than the ordinary materials entered into its composition. The interior of the tomb is very dimly illuminated from without, and the delicate beauty of its ornaments could scarcely be distinguished, were it not for the soft light thrown upon them by the brilliant lustre of this radiant canopy.

KING'S FORT,—BOORHANPORE.

Boorhanpore, in former times the capital of the province of Candeish, and the residence of the head of one of the Mahommedan powers established at an early period in the Deccan, is said to have been founded by a holy person of great pretensions, but of doubtful sanctity. Boorhan-ood-deen seems to have been one of those ambitious, subtle, and daring impostors, which Islamism has so often produced: he raised himself to great authority during his life-time, and since his death has been esteemed as a saint. His mausoleum at Rozah eclipses in splendour the imperial sepulchre of Aurungzebe, and far greater honours are paid to his memory. Lamps are still kept burning over the venerated dust, and his sarcophagus is canopied by a pall of green velvet—the sacred colour, which indicates that those who are permitted to use it, are either descendants of the Prophet, or have performed the pilgrimage to Mecca. The precincts of the building are the abode of Moollahs and other pious men, who are in daily attendance at the tomb; and upon great occasions, large nobuts, or drums, which are kept in one of the antechambers for the purpose, are beaten by the faithful, who thus commemorate the virtues, real and supposed, of the successful adventurer, who assumed the character of a prophet.

Boorhanpore, when under Moslem rule, was a large and flourishing place; it is situated in latitude 21° 16′ N. and longitude 76° 18′ E., on the north bank of the Taptee river, which rises in the province of Gundwana, and running westward nearly in a parallel line with the Nerbuddah, falls into the gulf of Cambay at Surat. This beautiful stream, which is fordable during the dry season, washes the walls of the picturesque ruins of the King's Fort, whose time-worn bastions and dilapidated ramparts are mirrored on the tranquil surface of its shining waters.

Vigorous even in its decay, though no longer formidable as a place of arms, the citadel of Boorhanpore, rising boldly from an elevated bank of the river, conveys to the spectator an idea of strength, which is not borne out upon a nearer inspection. Its vast tenantless courts are cumbered with huge fragments of ruins, and rank vegetation has found its way to the most secret recesses. The adjoining city is still populous, and considered to be one of the largest and best-built places in the Deccan. The greater number of the houses are of brick, handsomely ornamented, and a large proportion three stories in height; they are all covered with tiles, and, besides several streets wider and better paved than the generality of those to be found in Indian cities, there is a large chowk, or market-place, and an extensive thoroughfare called the Raj Bazar.

The remains of Mahommedan tombs and mosques in the neighbourhood shew that Boorhanpore was once the capital of a Moslem state. Its principal building, the Jumma Musjid, also bears evidence of the faith of its former rulers; it is a handsome edifice, constructed of grey stone, and crowned with lofty minarets. The followers of Boorhan, the reputed founder, are still very numerous; they constitute a peculiar sect of Mahommedans, now known by the denomination of Bohrah, who claim to be of Arabian origin, calling themselves Ishmeeliah, and deducing their religion from a disciple of Mahomet, who, in the age immediately succeeding that of the prophet, set up a creed of his own. It is said that they found their way into India through Guzerat, and it is certain that they still retain the characteristic features of the Arab countenance. They are a fine-looking set of people, and are distinguished from the rest of the inhabitants by a costume partaking of that worn in the country in which their ancestors are stated to have derived their extraction. They are men of active habits, and considerable wealth, acquired in mercantile pursuits. The best houses in the city are occupied by the Bohrahs, and they are celebrated all over this part of India for their attention to commerce, and the success with which it has been crowned.

After the decline of the Mahommedan empire in Hindoostan, Boorhanpore and its adjacencies fell under Mahratta sway. It, and the neighbouring fortress of Asseerghur, which has been justly styled the key of the Deccan, were among the first conquests of those splendid campaigns which, under Lord Lake, the Duke of Wellington and other well-known names in martial story subdued the formidable power which had arisen upon the ruin of the Mahommedan states, and which threatened to involve the whole of India in unremitting and devastating war. The territories which still groan under Mahratta rule, shew how cruel the fate of the peninsula would have been, had all its fair and fertile provinces become the prey of the most reckless, arbitrary, and selfish race of Eastern despots. Such a catastrophe would have been inevitable, but for the extraordinarily fortuitous circumstance which established a rival power in India, whose enterprise and success in war, and whose humane, mild, and wise government in peace, soon gave it an ascendance which can never be endangered except by the abandonment of those well-devised measures which secured its popularity.

The treaty of alliance with Dowlat Rao Scindrah, in 1804, (who, perceiving that he was no longer able to cope with the adversaries which the British arms raised up against him on every side, resorted to the old Mahratta policy of gaining time by negociations,) was signed at Boorhanpore. By the articles of this treaty, it was agreed to restore the city and the neighbouring fort of Asseerghur to its former ruler. Candeish had been originally a Mahratta province, and, after having been seized upon by successive Moslem

THE PASS OF MAKUNDRA.

dynasties, of Arab and Mogul descent, had reverted again to the children of the soil, whose right the British government recognized and respected. Though now secured from the desolating system pursued by Mahratta administrations, Candeish shews but too evident symptoms of having been long exposed to all the miseries of misrule. A great part of the country is waste and uncultivated, over-run with jungle, and abandoned to wild beasts. The villages are deserted and in ruins, and numerous aqueducts and dams, formerly in full activity, are no longer employed for the purpose of irrigation, but add by their dilapidated appearance to the melancholy aspect of the scene. The native tribes inhabiting Candeish are not likely, excepting under a very vigorous government, to improve the agricultural state of the country. They have not yet been weaned from their predatory habits, and prefer the exciting pursuit of game to the more peaceful occupation of tilling the soil. Yet, though addicted to forays, and preferring the capture of their neighbours' cattle to the trouble of rearing herds of their own, none of the freebooters who have figured in romance have acted more generously, or with truer notions of honour. It is no uncommon thing for young European officers, sent to act against the Bheels, to quit their outposts during the intervals of skirmishing, in order to enjoy a few days' sport with these accomplished hunters. They are invariably received with the greatest kindness, and in no instance have those tribes betrayed the confidence thus reposed in them. In fact, the secret of making the natives of India honest, is to trust them. Sir John Malcolm employed this expedient with great success; and there would be little danger in putting a notorious thief in charge of valuable property. The desire to retrieve a lost character would in most cases prevail over every other temptation; and though individuals, on whom the experiment has been tried, may not be thoroughly reclaimed, they seldom or ever prove unfaithful to their employers, and will respect *their* goods, while stealing from every body else.

MAKUNDRA MALWA.

The small, mean, but picturesque village of Makundra is beautifully situated in a valley of about three-quarters of a mile in diameter, and nearly of a circular form. Steep hills arise on every side, and there are only two openings, one to the south, and another to the north, each of which is defended by a stone wall and a gate, guarded by a small body of Chokeydars, belonging to the rajah of Kotah. This is the only pass for many miles through a ridge of mountains which divides Malwa from a small state inhabited by the Harrowtee tribe in Ajmere. Makundra is about eight and thirty miles from the large and populous city of Kotah, a place of considerable importance on the banks of the Chumbul. The scenery around it is exceedingly wild and beautiful, partaking of the characteristics of its neighbourhood; the rocky ledges, precipitous heights, and embowering trees, being diversified by a large jheel, or bowlee, reflecting on its glittering mirror the remains of tombs and temples, shadowed by magnificent groves, the haunts of wild peacocks. The water from this reservoir has not, however, a very good character; the natives impute to it some noxious qualities, and say that those who drink of it for the first time, are liable to fevers.

The pass of Makundra is celebrated, in the annals of British warfare, as the scene of an encounter between General Monson's brigade and Jeswunt Rao Holkar, during the retreat of the former, who, though offered shelter in the pass of Boondee by the rajah of that district, was afraid to trust to a prince of whose security he could not be assured. The valley of Boondee had too much the appearance of a trap, to permit the wary soldier to enter its (perchance) treacherous defile, and he preferred the chances of open warfare to so doubtful a security. The retrograde movement which Monson was compelled to make, though disastrous from the numerous obstacles presenting themselves in penetrating a wild and difficult country in the rainy season, has been accounted a masterly evolution, and one which reflects great credit upon the discipline and good conduct of the Indian army. Uninterrupted good fortune is, however, essential to secure the favourable opinion of the natives of the East; in the neighbourhood of Makundra, the retreat is spoken of as a flight to which some degree of disgrace may be attached. The inhabitants, in mentioning the affair with Holkar, state it to have happened at the time "when Monson ran away." Fortunately, the adjacent hills and passes have since resounded with the shouts of triumph under the conquering forces of General Donkin, who in this neighbourhood fell in with the van of Kurreem Khan's horde of Pindarries, and captured the chieftain's caparisoned elephant, his favourite wife, and all his baggage. The gallantry of the conquerors, of course, secured to the lady the highest degree of deference and respect, but the rest of Kurreem Khan's effects were speedily appropriated by the victors. The spoil underwent a very summary process, being sold by a sort of drum-head auction on the spot, and the proceeds divided among the party assembled—the most certain as well as the quickest method of securing prize-money.

To return, however, to Monson: Although he did not avail himself of the offer made to him by the Boondian rajah, the British government rewarded the apparent good faith of its ally by an increase of territory. Could implicit confidence have been placed, in these treacherous times, in professions which unfortunately were but too often of the most deceitful nature, Monson's luckless detachment would have been spared all the accumulated horrors of the march to Agra. Disappointed in the hope of finding an asylum at Kotah, and harassed by repeated attacks from Holkar's troops, they arrived at length at a place of security, in a state of the utmost distress. All had been lost save their honour, which they had upheld nobly in several actions, sustained against fearful odds, with a force flushed with victory, and greatly outnumbering their own.

Makundra has subsequently been the theatre of Pindarree warfare, and the haunt of Bheel robbers, and other wild predatory tribes, inhabitants of the hills, who, like the generality of mountaineers, consider plundering to be their lawful occupation. Since the dispersion and subjection of the Pindarrees, and the entire settlement of Malwa and its adjacencies, this celebrated thoroughfare has become the scene of murders still more appalling than those formerly perpetrated by the armed and mounted freebooters, who galloped into a village, and put to the sword all who were unable to effect their escape from the sudden and furious onslaught. The Pindarrees at least waged open warfare, and travellers acquainted with their danger provided against it by assembling in large bodies, and furnishing themselves with weapons of defence. In the apparently peaceable state in which the country reposed after the Pindarree war, these precautions were abandoned, and solitary travellers, or small parties, set forward upon long journeys unaware that their path was beset by assassins, from whom scarcely any degree of poverty formed a protection.

It appears from the most authentic documents, that the whole of the upper provinces of Hindoostan swarm with a class of banditti called Thugs, or Phansegars, from their dexterity in strangling. These men have secret signs, by which they become known to each other while mingling in communities perfectly unsuspicious of the desperate courses in which they are engaged. During a part of the year they remain quietly in their own homes, engaged in cultivating the land, but at the end of the rainy season each village sends out its gang; and parties, of from ten or a dozen to thirty, collect together, and, in the guise of travellers, pursue their way towards the central provinces. They are totally without weapons, and are careful to avoid every appearance which might excite alarm; the instrument with which they perpetrate their murders being nothing more than a strip of cloth. While journeying along the high roads, they mark out all whom they may fall in with for destruction, who do not present a very formidable appearance; following their victims for several days, until they come to a place in which they may conveniently effect their purpose. In lonely parts of the country, very little time is lost. A select number of the band go forward, and dig the graves; those who have attained the requisite dexterity in strangling, slip the cloth round the necks of the doomed, who are stripped in an instant, and carried off to the place of interment. In more populous districts, greater precaution is used. The murder is generally deferred until night-fall, and the custom adopted in India. of bivouacking in the open air, greatly facilitates the designs of the murderers.

Travellers usually carry along with them the materials for their simple repast; they kindle fires on the ground, prepare their cakes of meal, and sit down to the enjoyment of their pipes. The Thugs, who employ the most insinuating arts to entice persons pursuing the same route to join their company, appear to be employed in the same preparations, but at a given signal, generally some common and familiar word, such as "bring tobacco," the work of death commences, often in full view of some neighbouring village. Nothing, however, occurs which could give a distant spectator an idea of the tragic scene enacting before his eyes: one or two persons are singing and playing on the tomtom, in order to impart an air of careless festivity to the group, and to stifle any cry which might escape the victims. The murders are simultaneously performed upon all the party marked out for destruction, and the dim and fast-fading twilight involves the whole scene in impenetrable obscurity. The bodies are hastily deposited in the ground; and fires are immediately kindled upon the graves, to prevent the traces of newly turned earth from being discernible. When the accumulation of booty becomes considerable, a detachment is sent off with it to some convenient depôt, where it is sold, or otherwise disposed of, for the benefit of the captors. Pedestrian travellers frequently carry valuable property about with them, both in money and ornaments, and, as appearances are often exceedingly deceitful, the Thugs make no distinction, seizing upon those who bear the marks of poverty as well as upon persons of substance accompanied by baggage and attendants. They are careful not to attack the inhabitants of a place through which they may pass, as a person missing from a village would lead to detection.

The immense distance which wayfarers in India traverse to the place of their destination, the slowness of their method of travelling, where there are no public conveyances, or relays of cattle, and men and horsemen only accomplish one, or at most two stages, per diem, and the various impediments which may detain them more than the usual period upon the road, are very favourable to the designs of the Thugs. Months may elapse after the victims of these assassins have mouldered in their graves, before any suspicion of their untimely fate has risen in the minds of their relatives.

The Thugs have many agents and abettors amongst the inferior members of the police, who furnish them with important intelligence, and use the most artful endeavours to explain away appearances which tend to criminate them. During many years they carried on their fearful trade without exciting in the neighbouring community more than a vague suspicion of their existence: their habits and modes of living, though known to and reported by some active servants of the Government, after a time, in the frequent changes of the magistrates, ceased to excite attention, or to become the subject of inquiry. Lately, however, large masses of information relative to the profession of Thuggy have come to light; and we may hope that the publicity given to the conviction of detected criminals will put travellers upon their guard.

THE INTERIOR OF THE BISMA KURM,—CAVES OF ELLORA.

Amidst the numerous objects of attraction at Ellora, the grand Bhood cave, known by the name of the Bisma Kurm, or Visvacarma, produces, from its massive simplicity, the unity of its design, and the magnitude of its proportions, the strongest impressions upon the mind. It is the only large temple at Ellora which has been excavated with an arched roof; and the lofty vaulted ceiling, the solid octagonal pillars, and the grave character of the figures which are sculptured upon and above the architrave, combine to fill the soul with a feeling of religious awe, which cannot be inspired by the fantastic, though spirited, representations of the objects of Brahminical worship.

A colossal image of Boodh appears at the end of the noble vista, of which a perspective view is given in the accompanying plate; the dignity and repose of this figure add greatly to the solemn effect of the long-vaulted aisle, and the dim religious light which sheds its solemn hues upon the scene. Placed in obscurity, its gigantic form indistinctly revealed through the sober twilight of the cave, no idol made by men's hands could so strongly convey the notions we have formed of the mysterious grandeur, the awful power, and terrible majesty of the Deity; and in the absence of the true light, we can scarcely wonder, that, thus typified, thousands and tens of thousands have bowed the knee to Baal.

INTERIOR OF THE BISMA KURM, CAVES OF ELLORA.

JAHARA BAUG, — AGRA.

Although the Hindoos admit that there is only one God, and are unanimous in declaring the numerous personages of their mythology to be merely emanations from the one great Source of truth, it is difficult to maintain this creed in the midst of the multitudinous variety of forms under which the Creator, in his almost innumerable characters, is worshipped.

The attendant Brahmins entitle the Bisma Kurm, the "Carpenter's Cave," and say that it was the work of a grandson of Brahma, who belonged to the caste of mechanics in wood: he had the honour of being employed as the architect by Vishnu himself; and, according to the popular opinion, he has perpetuated the remembrance of his fellow-labourers, by placing them over the entablature on which the principal figures rest—a situation which enables them to view with great complacency the result of their honourable toil. Every visiter to Ellora is amused by the extraordinary conceits and strange legends related by the Brahmins who loiter about the caves; but no reliance can be placed upon traditional tales, evidently of modern origin, and invented long after Budhism had declined in this part of Asia. For all accurate and authentic information, we must refer to the accounts printed by the few learned persons who have made these interesting antiquities the subject of their study; and though too often quoted to afford any new light, we must be again indebted to the report of Captain Sykes, for the only description of this temple which can be securely relied upon. "This cave," he tells us, "is eighty feet long by forty-two and a half broad, measuring from wall to wall of the side aisles; the height is thirty-five feet six inches. The extreme depth of the excavation into the hill from the outer gate, is a hundred and sixty-six feet. There are twenty-eight octangular pillars in two rows, besides two pillars supporting a gallery over the door-way. A narrow border, or architrave, immediately above the pillars, which runs all around the cave, is filled with human figures, male and female. Above this is a broader border, or frieze, divided into compartments; in each of which is a sitting figure of Boodh, with four attendants: projecting over this border are prostrate human figures by way of cornice, alternately male and female; and the end of each of the ribs of the roof appears to rest upon the back of one of these figures."

JAHARA BAUG,—AGRA.

The eastern bank of the river Jumna, at Agra, is adorned by a succession of beautiful gardens of great luxuriance and vast extent, where the orange, the citron, and the vine are the richest and fairest of fruit; where the air is refreshed by fountains, and where marble pavilions offer rest and repose to those who delight to revel in all the pomp of Oriental luxury. The Jahara-bang, or garden, is the name given to one of these delightful retreats; and in wandering through its stately avenues, the readers of the Arabian tales see the vivid picture realized, which imagination has painted, of the imperial pleasure-grounds on the banks of the Tigris, the scene of the adventures of Haroun Alraschid, with Noureddin Ali, and the fair Persian.

Nothing can be more enchanting than the view which is presented from the pavilion represented in the plate, erected on the extreme point of a small peninsula, and overhanging the river. The Jumna flows over a rocky bed; its bright, smooth, and sparkling sands are the haunt of the loveliest of the feathered tribes: small white herons, and delicate pink-plumaged birds, are seen dipping and hovering around; while the trees, obtruding into the stream, and flinging down their rich flowery garlands into the water, are tenanted with innumerable tribes of green pigeons, ring-necked paroquets, or yellow-breasted bayas.

On the opposite bank, one of the most beautiful cities in Hindoostan spreads its architectural splendours in the richest profusion before the admiring gazer; the marble palace of Shah Jehan glitters on the very edge of the water; its terraces, turrets, and pinnacles reflected in the bright mirror which stretches itself below. In the back ground, the bastioned walls and massive gateways of the city appear crowned with the shining cupolas of the pearl mosque, and partially concealed by the shading foliage of the neem, the peepul, and the tamarind-tree; the long and beautiful perspective of tower, palace, ghaut, and embowering grove, closed by the tall minars and lofty dome of the Tâj Mahal.

Nothing short of a panoramic view can convey an adequate idea of the multiplicity of beautiful objects which rivet the gaze in this extensive and magnificent prospect, or the imposing effect which it produces when seen at the moment in which the rising sun bathes the whole scene in one bright flood of gold.

The bendings and turnings of the river afford, from flowery promontories similar to that represented in the plate, a perpetual succession of views; but from the minarets of Etemad-ud-Dowlat's tomb, situated in the immediate neighbourhood, the eye takes in the wide and richly varied prospect, many miles in extent, at a single glance. This building, which stands in the midst of a wilderness near the Jahara Baug, is by many esteemed the most chaste and beautiful specimen of architecture which the Moghuls have bequeathed to the land of their adoption. It was erected by the celebrated Nour Mahal, over the remains of her father. The beautiful favourite, it is said, originally intended to construct the mausoleum raised to the memory of her beloved parent, of solid silver, but abandoned the design at the suggestion of a judicious friend, who assured her that marble would be more durable.

Compared with many of the sepulchral monuments of India, the tomb of Etemad-ud-Dowlah is small: it consists of one central hall, with octagonal apartments at the angles, surmounted by a dome, and four open minarets. The whole building is covered with a lattice of marble, adorned with flowers and foliage, forming a rich mosaic inlay of the most exquisite workmanship. Unfortunately, hitherto this beautiful mausoleum has not attracted the attention of the Government; there are no funds appropriated to its repair, and it exhibits marks of decay, which, if not speedily arrested, will, in the course of a very few years, effect its utter desolation. The walls of the surrounding garden have been broken down; and the herbage, now spreading over the neglected parterres, afford a scanty pasturage to a few stray cows: we may hope, however, that the impending ruin may be averted by the influx of Europeans of wealth and influence, which the elevation of Agra into a seat of government will bring to its walls.

SEVEN-STORIED PALACE, BEJAPORE.

SEVEN-STORIED PALACE,—BEJAPORE.

The beautiful remains of this once splendid palace, of which a distant view has been given in a preceding plate, arise within the walls of the fortified portion of Bejapore. The architecture differs considerably from that of the numerous ruins which attract the eye in this interesting city; it is lighter and of a more graceful character, its airy elegance contrasting finely with the massive solemnity of the mosques and tombs around.

Very few Eastern cities have the advantage of so much variety in the style of their buildings, as is to be found at Bejapore; a circumstance to be accounted for by the great admixture of foreigners at the court of its former princes, who were of Turkish descent. The greater portion of the nobility were composed of Persians, Turks, and Tartars, who, in all probability, introduced novelties from the countries of their birth; and we are told by Ferishta, that the first sovereign of the Adil Shah dynasty invited several eminent artists, belonging to distant lands, to assist in the decorations of the city, and "made them easy under the shade of his bounty." The remains of the carved work and gilding, still to be found in the interior of the seven-storied palace, afford beautiful specimens of the state of the art at the period of its erection; but there is no authentic record extant to acquaint us by whom this splendid building was constructed, though there is abundance of reason to suppose that it was the residence of Yusuf Adil Shah himself.

The history of the founder of a kingdom, once the most flourishing and powerful in the Deccan, is of a very interesting and romantic nature. He was, it is said, a son of the emperor Bajazet, and according to the policy of Eastern courts, which permits no younger brother near the throne, was destined by the reigning monarch to be put to death. Agreeably to the sovereign's mandate, the executioners came to demand the young prince, then a mere boy, of his mother, in order that, having strangled him, the body might be publicly exposed. The unhappy lady, after vainly entreating the remission of this cruel decree, obtained a delay of four-and-twenty hours to prepare her mind for the loss which she was doomed to sustain, and immediately sent into the slave market to purchase a substitute for her son. An unfortunate Circassian boy, who bore some resemblance to the prince, was selected for the victim, and, prevailing upon one of the ministers to favour the deceit, he suffered the fate intended for another, and by this humane expedient, the queen succeeded in saving the life of her youngest born.

The persons to whose care prince Yusuf was entrusted carried him to a place of security, whither he remained until he was sixteen years old, when, through the garrulity of his nurse, the secret of his birth having transpired, he wandered into Persia. A remarkable dream, which occurred to him while residing at Shiraz, determined him to try his fortune in India, where he was assured that he should attain to sovereign power. Fortune smiled upon his enterprise. He arose to some eminence under the governor of Berar, and, upon the dissolution of the Bhamanee empire in the Deccan, he resolved to push his fortune, and as in the words of his historian Ferishta, the hooma* of prosperity had spread the shadow of his wings over his head, he became master of a rich and fertile territory, and established himself as a sovereign at Bejapore. Upon the marriage of his daughter, the Beeby Musseety, with Prince Ahmed at Koolburga, that princess took her seat above all the other ladies of the court; and, upon being remonstrated with, replied, that as the daughter of Yusuf Adil Shah, and the niece and grand-daughter of two emperors of Rome, she considered herself to be inferior to no lady in the Deccan. It is said that the truth of this assertion was established upon inquiry at Constantinople, and the claims of the noble lady to pre-eminence was thenceforth allowed at the court of her father-in-law.

Gibbon mentions the fact of Mahomed having, on his accession, ordered all his brothers to be put to death, and states also in a note, that one of them was saved, and became a Christian. The elegant and erudite translator of Ferishta's history appears to think it possible that another also might have escaped, whose adventures, in consequence of the distant theatre of action, must have been perfectly unknown to European historians; under the authority of such a sanction, we may therefore venture to give credit to the tale of Yusuf's birth and preservation.

Ferishta, unfortunately, is rather sparing of domestic anecdotes, the events which he relates respecting the kingdom of Bejapore, being little more than a series of disturbances, rebellions, and conspiracies, yet the architectural remains testify that the resources of the state must not only have been very extensive, but also very frequently expended upon works of considerable public utility. The aqueducts, tanks, and wells, still in existence, and which have been mentioned in former pages of this work, prove that the taste for useless splendour and posthumous fame, so remarkably exemplified in the tombs of Hindoostan, and so strongly displayed at Bejapore, was mingled with a desire to confer a lasting benefit upon posterity. A well-informed person, a descendant of one of the hoozoors of the ancient kings, who acted as guide to Captain Sykes during his visit, averred that there were still in tolerable preservation at Bejapore, "seven hundred wells with steps, three hundred without steps, seven hundred mosques and tombs of stone, and seven hundred of bricks and chunam;" and those who have visited the city, and beheld the multitude of its buildings, and the amazing extent of ground which they cover, do not refuse to give credit to the assertion.

Many of the most interesting reliques of Bejapore are so little injured by the neglect and devastation which have converted the surrounding country into a wilderness, as to give a hope that they may survive to be the ornaments of another capital, far happier and better governed than that which fell into dust under the stern despotism of Aurungzebe, and the wild vengeance of the Mahrattas.

* It is fabled of this bird, that whoever comes under the shadow of his wings will wear a crown. Mr. Neave, in describing the attributes of this king-maker, supposes that our idea of the phœnix has been taken from the hooma of Eastern story, and adds, that, judging from the number of kings at present in India, they must be very rare indeed, more especially in the Honourable Company's territories, where it would be difficult to find a single nest.

While wandering amongst the ruins of Bejapore, the moralist may reflect upon the certain consequences of overweening ambition—the defeat of the most cherished objects of a despot's soul, by the very means which he has taken to secure their success. Aurungzebe, in overthrowing the independent kingdoms of Hindoostan, and dethroning their princes in order to become the sole and sovereign ruler of the Mahommedan empire, weakened the barriers which opposed themselves to the growing power of the Mahrattas, and paved the way to the final destruction of the Moghul dynasty. The descendant of this unrelenting victor sits upon the frail remnant of a throne, snatched from the clutch of the Mahrattas by the bayonets of a foreign power; and the present state of Bejapore will serve to shew what the destiny of India would have been, had not the ascendency of the British government secured it from becoming subject to Mahratta rule.

The numerous vicissitudes to which the city of Bejapore has been subjected has given rise to an idea that immense treasures in gold and jewels are secreted amidst its ruins. The custom of burying money is still very prevalent in India; this expedient being not only resorted to in troublous times, but also finding favour with avaricious persons who are unwilling that their successors should benefit by their wealth. Runjeet Sing is said to have been seized by a passion for accumulating and for burying money; and we are told that the Begum Sumroo secretes four lacs a year in this manner. It is, therefore, not surprising that there should be persons at Bejapore willing to give large sums for the privilege of digging and delving under some old wall. This is a favourite speculation amongst the natives; and many are deluded, both of their time and their money, by the expectation of finding incalculable riches amidst the foundations of the deserted city.

It is to be hoped that the remains of the seven-storied palace may be saved from the researches of these treasure seekers; though, as the building has already suffered more from the injuries which time and war have brought upon Bejapore than its immediate neighbours, ruin has now advanced too far to be arrested. As it has been before observed, those who have visited the city are struck with the freshness and unimpaired strength of many of the buildings, compared with the prevailing character of decay and desolation. They say that the city in some parts exhibits such a wild waste of ruin, that it seems scarcely credible that so much destruction could have been effected by man's neglect in the ordinary course of time, but rather that some violent convulsion of nature must have caused this mighty, terrible, yet partial devastation. And this idea seems to be borne out by the numberless beautiful and massive remains which have escaped the fearful havoc, and which, still exhibiting the noblest specimens of architecture, give promise of almost endless durability. A great part of the gilding has not lost its first gloss, and the elaborate ornaments of many of the exteriors retain their minute and exquisite degree of finish wholly unimpaired.

DUS AWTAR—CAVES OF ELLORA.

The name by which this excavation is distinguished is said, by the Brahmins in attendance, to be derived from the representations of the ten incarnations, or avatars of Vishnoo, sculptured in the several compartments around it. The cave occurs in the centre of the range, and the learned have decided that it has no claim to this particular appellation, since all its Brahminical neighbours are equally supplied with delineations of the exploits of the god during his sojourn in this nether world. The subject of the accompanying plate is taken from one of the most perfect remains of the numerous compartments. It represents Siva, who forms the principal figure, in the act of punishing the audacity of a demon guilty of offering an insult to Parwutee, who, in his character of Ehr Budr, he had espoused. There is so little interest in Brahminical fable, that the mere stories attached to these spirited sculptures can only engage the attention of learned men; the casual spectator loses all curiosity respecting the adventures of the Hindoo gods, in the pleasure to be derived in the contemplation of the wondrous scene chosen by the followers of Brahma and of Bhood for the worship of their deities.

The Dus Awtar, though evidently, from the multitude of its figures, actively engaged in the affairs of life, a Brahminical temple is distinguished from other excavations of the same description by having cells opening into one of its halls, resembling those which are found in the Buddhist caves; figures, in the attitudes assumed by Bhood, adorn the capitals of the pillars in front, and visiters are puzzled and perplexed by the amicable admixture of two religions which have for so long a period been at variance with each other. The most diligent inquirer has not ventured to decide which of the two hostile sects possesses the strongest claim to antiquity; it is, however, a curious fact, that the Nerbuddah, a river dedicated to Bhood, and still bearing his name, is considered to this day by the Hindoos to be of a more sacred character than the Ganges. It is necessary, they say, that a man should taste of the Ganges before he can derive any advantage from its waters, but that the sight of the Nerbuddah is sufficient to purify him; and while the inhabitants of the provinces through which the Ganges takes its course are reconciled to the slaughter of oxen upon its banks, those in the vicinity of the Nerbuddah attribute all the calamities which have ruined their harvests to the consumption of beef by Christian and Mahomedan troops stationed in the neighbourhood of that holy river. Crimes, they say, in such a place, were always visited more immediately and severely than elsewhere; and though they had at first imagined that the failure of their crops was occasioned by the indifference of the British government to feminine derelictions, the second marriages of the widows of Rajpoots and Brahmins, they were now convinced that the vengeance of heaven had been aroused by the horrible sacrifice of the sacred animal. Trees were pointed out, which had been withered in consequence of having had joints of beef hung upon their branches while the British troops were stationed in the adjacent cantonments, and none could be persuaded that such a visitation was the natural consequence of a severe frost.

DUS AWTAR, CAVES OF ELLORA.

VIEW ON A RIVER NEAR CANTON.

The compartment represented in the engraving occurs in the upper story of the Dus Awtar, in a chamber ninety-eight feet in breadth, and one hundred and two feet deep. It has a flat roof nearly twelve feet in height, and supported by forty-eight massive pillars, in addition to twenty-two pilasters along the walls, dividing the several compartments or niches, containing the sculptures, from each other. The whole façade in front is open, admitting a more than usual portion of light, and shewing off the interior embellishments to great advantage.

A VIEW ON A SMALL RIVER NEAR CANTON.

The view represented in the accompanying plate, which occurs upon one of the tributary streams of the Tigris, near Canton, presents a very accurate specimen of the scenery to be found along the banks of the Chinese rivers. The houses upon either side are inhabited by artisans, the most ingenious and industrious of their race. The curious methods by which these people contrive to gain a subsistence afford great amusement to the stranger, who views with astonishment the persevering labours and extraordinary devices employed by a redundant population to obtain the means of existence.

It will be seen by the accompanying plate, that the banks of the Chinese rivers are low, and that their interest is derived solely from the luxuriance of the cultivation, the neatness of the clustering cottages overhung by the graceful bamboo, and the vivid tints of the flowers and the foliage. The landscape is at intervals diversified by high grounds in the distance, but these are frequently of a cheerless appearance, being bare and of a sterile aspect, affording a strong and disagreeable contrast to the excessive fertility of the plains. Rice plantations are very frequent on the banks of the rivers; the sugar-cane is also extensively cultivated; amongst the vegetable curiosities are the pith plants, from which the Chinese manufacture the paper so closely resembling velvet, commonly used for drawings; and the *conchorus*, from which the fine grass cloth is made, a texture nearly as beautiful and far more durable than French cambric, both of which, there is every reason to believe, might be brought to flourish in a European soil. One of the principal objects of attraction, and one also of frequent recurrence in the neighbourhood of Canton, is the *duck-boat*, in which the keeper and breeder of the ducks, with his family, take up their residence, inhabiting huts or cabins erected upon the deck, while the feathered tribes are accommodated in the hold below. These boats shift their stations continually in search of places in which the ducks may find the most abundant supply of food, and are most frequently to be seen in the neighbourhood of the rice-fields, from which, after the grain has been cut, a plentiful harvest remains for broad-billed birds, these animals growing fat amid the stubble. When the boat is moored to some convenient spot, it is connected to the shore by means of a plank, along which the ducks take their waddling march, making straight for the places offering the best prospect of indulging their voracious appetites. They do not, however, quit their floating habitation until they hear the accustomed whistle. After their keepers suppose that they have had sufficient time to feed, a second whistle warns them to return. Knowing the danger of delay, they instantly make the best of their way home; the first bird is received with caresses, and even rewarded by an additional feed, while the unfortunate last in the race is punished with a whipping. This expedient effectually prevents all loitering upon the road, and almost incredible efforts are made by the rear-guard to exchange their situation with the van of the army,—many endeavour to fly over the backs of their comrades, and all evince the greatest anxiety to escape the inevitable doom attendant on the laggard. The floating habitations of the river are usually kept very neatly, and the cleanliness which prevails gives a cheerful air to the ragged families crowded in such narrow space, and, in despite of their extreme poverty, they appear to be happy and contented. There is something, however, exceedingly disgusting in the aspect of the articles exhibited for sale as human food—cats, dogs, rats, &c. appearing with more legitimate subjects for the table.

To judge from a very interesting work lately published,* the merits of Chinese gardening have been a good deal overrated. Mr. Bennett assures us, that the boasted Fa-tee gardens, which are situated near Canton on the opposite bank of the river, do not by any means equal the least distinguished of our provincial nursery grounds; yet the splendour of the Chinese flowers is not to be surpassed, and infinite varieties might be obtained by a little attention to their cultivation. The Chinese appear to be more anxious to produce objects of curiosity than of interest; their dwarf trees, therefore, form the principal attraction of their gardens. These plants afford perfect, though Lilliputian specimens of the monarchs of the forests; and elms, bamboos, and other umbrageous trees, apparently of ancient growth, and having all the characteristics of the largest species, may be seen only a few inches in height, and springing out of the smallest pots. The process by which this result is obtained is not very difficult. A young and healthy branch is, in the first instance, taken from a large tree; the bark is stripped off, and its place supplied by a mixture of clay and chopped straw. When the roots appear, they are cut off and transplanted; the shoots which they throw out are trained in a particular manner, and both these and the roots kept so closely clipped and confined, that their growth is effectually checked, various methods being employed to produce this effect. An appearance of age is given to the trunk by boring holes in it, and smearing it over with sugar. The ants speedily find their way to the tempting food; and when they have completed their depredations, the tree seems to have survived a hundred storms. It is necessary to repeat the clipping and cutting at intervals, in order to keep down the luxuriance of nature; and perhaps the most curious of these productions are the dwarf orange trees, which appear laden with fruit of the most diminutive size. The Chinese appear to take the greatest delight in raising wonder by the untiring patience with which they overcome difficulties, which to less persevering people would amount to impossibilities. Their dwarf trees, their ivory balls, and many other varieties of the same nature, are rather curious than useful; but they frequently exercise the same skill and patience to more profitable purposes, in the improvement of articles of general utility. The splendour of the Chinese colours excites universal admiration; and it is a curious fact, that although they are not able

* Wanderings in New South Wales, Batavia, Pedir Coast, Singapore, and China. By George Bennett, Esq.

RUINS ABOUT THE TAJ MAHAL,-AGRA.

to manufacture the original pigment so well as it is made in Europe, and therefore import their best paints, yet by washing each colour in a hundred waters, and submitting to other toilsome expedients, they succeed in producing that matchless brilliance of hue which is so vainly sought after at home. The desire to obtain this gorgeousness of artificial colouring was doubtless suggested by the wish to imitate the superb tints in the plumage of the birds, and the petals of the flowers, which render the natural productions of China the most magnificent in the world. It is only lately that the testimony of eye-witnesses has proved the existence of that splendid variety of golden carp, which was supposed to have owed the greater portion of its beauty to the fancy of the delineator, but which is to be found in the lakes of southern China. Ponds of gold and silver fish are the common ornaments of great men's gardens; they are covered after sunset with a gauze frame, to protect them from the various enemies seeking their destruction under the shadow of the night, though, notwithstanding the care which is taken for their preservation, they sometimes become the prey of the kingfisher.

RUINS ABOUT THE TAJ MAHAL, AGRA.

The former extent and splendour of the city of Agra may be traced by the number of the ruins which spread themselves around upon every side. Vast tracts covered with old buildings, the remains of wells, and fragments of walls, which originally flourished in the midst of verdure, and under the shade of forest trees, now only render the wide waste of sand, which has swallowed up all vegetation, still more desolate. The country between the fort of Agra and the Taj Mahal is a perfect desert; and visitors, after winding their way through an arid plain, only diversified by sand-heaps and crumbling masses of stone, come, as if by enchantment, upon the luxuriant gardens which still adorn the mausoleum where Nour Jehan and the beautiful partner of his throne sleep in undisturbed repose.

The marble cupola seen to the left of the plate, crowns a beautiful musjid or mosque, attached to the Taj; beyond, flanked by its slender minars, the Taj itself appears; and in the distance the eye rests upon the cupolas and turrets of the magnificent gateway which forms the principal entrance of this terrestrial paradise. Constant irrigation is necessary in India to preserve the beauty of gardens, which soon disappears if not continually refreshed by the revivifying stream. The pleasure-grounds belonging to the Taj Mahal are watered daily during the dry season; and they are clothed in perpetual verdure, while the surrounding country is a wilderness.

The arched gateway represented in the plate, leads into an enclosure of considerable extent, intervening between the plain and the gardens of the Taj. Many buildings of the same nature skirt these beautiful gardens, and some have been fitted up for the residencies of European families during the rains, the only season in which native habitations, however splendid, can be easily converted into comfortable abodes for strangers, from a colder country; it being both difficult to exclude the hot winds, and to warm chambers, open to every breath of heaven, sufficiently during the cold weather. The natives themselves are content to envelop their persons in thick clothing; the men wear several shawls, and the women put on wadded garments and extra veils, during a period in which the English residents shut up their doors and windows and sit around fires.

The superior elegance of the native architecture renders it a subject for regret, that so few of the deserted buildings, in the neighbourhood of British cantonments, should have been adapted to the use of the new comers: one or two of the mosques and tombs of Agra have been fitted up for the reception of the families of resident civilians; but the greater number of the European population are lodged in excessively ugly bungalows, built with the old bricks which cover miles of the suburbs of Agra, and which may be had for the trouble of fetching them. A few of the newly-constructed houses are in better taste, after the Italian manner; but these occur too seldom to atone for the frightful and barnlike appearance of the rest. The gardens attached to these houses, though large, luxuriant, and well planted, are too much isolated from them to improve their general aspect; and the only attempt to beautify the tract exclusively occupied by military residents in the close neighbourhood of the Taj Mahal, has been made by the introduction of Parkinsonias. These trees, originally imported from the Cape by Colonel Parkinson, thrive well, with very little attention, in the most arid spots. When mingled with others, they would be very attractive, but their leaves being entirely obscured by an abundance of bright yellow flowers, their effect, when scattered singly over a sandy plain, is any thing rather than pleasing. The court and council of the new presidency will find much to do upon their arrival at Agra, and there is fortunately abundance of material for the exercise of taste and talent.

The church belonging to the cantonments is a very handsome structure, built under the superintendence of an officer of engineers. Several excellent architects are to be found in this department of the service, and Agra is much indebted to the gentleman who has held an appointment for some years in the board of works at that station, for the improvements which he has introduced into the interiors of the bungalows built under his direction. The necessity of consulting economy, and of excluding the heat, have exceedingly injured the outward appearance of Anglo-Indian residences in the province; but though, at Agra, both the brick and the *enteha* houses (the name given to those constructed of unbaked mud) are miracles of ugliness, many of the interiors are finished with great elegance. The best boast of chimney-pieces of marble chunam, and the walls are decorated with mouldings and cornices, which take away from the bleak and desolate air usually the characteristics of these unsophisticated edifices. A great deal, however, still remains to be done; and although military residents have not very extensive funds at their disposal, should a spirit of emulation be created amongst them, they will at least plant out what it may be impossible to pull down and rebuild, and thus render the cantonments of Agra more worthy of their beautiful neighbour, the Taj Mahal.

MAH CHUNG KEOW,-CANTON.

MAH CHUNG KEOW

The peculiar beauty of the Chinese bridge, and its adaptation for the purpose of ornamental embellishment to landscape gardening, have long ago occasioned its introduction into English parks and pleasure-grounds. The elegant specimen afforded by the accompanying plate occurs in the immediate neighbourhood of Canton. It spans a stream which falls into the river on the side opposite to that whereon the city is built, and within the narrow limits permitted by a jealous government to be perambulated by European strangers.

There are few places in which inland navigation is carried on to a greater extent than in China. The Imperial, or Grand Canal, is a work of unparalleled magnitude, and the city of Canton might be styled the Venice of the East, on account of its being intersected in every direction by artificial rivulets. The bulky portion of the merchandise is conveyed to every part of the city by water. A large canal extends along the whole length of the eastern side, another takes a westerly direction; between these two, and communicating with each, there is a third canal, which nearly skirts the wall on the north side, so that boats can pass to and fro, from one to the other. The suburbs are also supplied with several canals, and from these large channels, a great number of smaller ones flow, which are called by the Chinese, "the veins of the city." The bridges are numerous; many of them are constructed of stone, and, like the one represented in the engraving, contribute not a little to the picturesqueness of the landscape.

There is some difficulty in ascertaining the precise extent of Canton, the Chinese themselves differing in their accounts of it. Some late European visitants, in making the circuit of the walls, have walked the whole distance in little less than two hours; and, according to their calculation, they cannot exceed six English miles in circumference. The walls are constructed partly of stone, and partly of brick; the former, which is chiefly coarse sand-stone, is employed in the foundation and lower portion of the walls, the arch-ways, and the gates; the bricks are very small, and of a soft texture, the economy necessary in the article of fuel preventing them from being more than half baked. In several places, particularly along the eastern side, time and the warfare of the elements have made such serious inroads, that in the event of an attack from experienced engineers, they would offer a very feeble defence, and could not stand an instant before a besieging army directed by European skill. They are nearly perpendicular in their elevation, and vary in height from twenty-five to thirty-five, or forty feet: they do not exceed twenty-five feet in thickness, and in some places not more than twenty. They are the strongest and most formidable on the northern side, the quarter from which hostility is chiefly to be dreaded: a line of battlements extends all round on the summit of the walls, and there are embrasures at intervals: altogether, the whole, though imposing to the eye, is totally deficient in the strength requisite to withstand the artillery of modern times. There are sixteen gates, but as four of them are opened through the wall which separates the old city from the new one, there are only twelve entrances to the outer erection. The suburbs of Canton are very extensive on three sides of the city, spreading themselves to the east over the whole interval between the walls and the river: towards the north, however, there are only a few scattered huts of the meanest description. The streets of Canton are very numerous, more than six hundred being enumerated in the catalogues published by the natives. Some are long, and handsome, but the greater portion short, narrow, and exceedingly crooked; they vary in breadth from two to sixteen feet, but the greater number are about six or eight feet wide, and all are flagged with large stones, chiefly granite: some of the names are very fanciful—the dragon, the flying dragon, and the martial dragon street, the flower, the golden flower, and the golden street, appear amid others of less note. The houses present an infinite variety of architecture, though few are upon a very grand or splendid scale. The principal material is brick, but two-fifths may be said to be of mud, the houses of the Tartars inhabiting the old city being all of this description. Stone and wood are not very extensively employed, but the former is used in the construction of gate-ways and door-posts; and columns, beams, and rafters are formed of the latter: the floors of the best mansions are paved with marble; in those of inferior splendour, thin tiles are used; but the greater number are composed of indurated mud: few are supplied with glass windows, the substitutes being oiled paper, mica, or shell.

Bricks are manufactured in the neighbourhood of Canton, and brought into the city in boats; they are chiefly of a pale brown, or lead colour, those only that have been thoroughly burned being red: the brown are merely baked in the sun; and the blue, though submitted to the kiln, are not allowed to remain long enough to become hardened, or of a deep colour; they are sold at from three to eight dollars a thousand. The greater number of the houses belonging to the most respectable inhabitants are enclosed in a wall twelve or fourteen feet in height, which completely conceals the interior from the view of the passenger. The outer gate opens into a small court, or ornamented garden, and along the front of the mansion the reception hall extends, which is frequently only enclosed upon three sides, having nothing but a row of pillars towards the court. These apartments are very neatly fitted up, and supplied with those light and pretty articles of furniture in which the Chinese excel. The grandeur of the superior habitations is displayed more in extent than in elevation, but their numerous courts and avenues do not exhibit long colonnades or noble quadrangles, being cut up into petty details, and having more of grotesqueness than of elegance in their effect. The handsomest buildings are those belonging to the different hongs, or factories, established by foreign nations,—that of the English East India Company being finer, and of greater extent, than the whole of the others.

A great part of the city and suburbs is built upon low ground, and flats near the river; and in situations of this description, where the soil is loose and muddy, the houses are raised upon wooden piles, which are necessary to render the foundations secure; some of these appear above the ground, and the edifices erected upon them are of slight materials, principally wood, but in others the piles are surmounted a few feet below the surface by a foundation of mud, brick, or stone, and in these cases the building is completed in the same manner: many are entirely baseless, and during heavy floods these wretched habitations are completely carried away.

The shops are gaily painted, and fitted up with great attention to convenience and comfort, with lacquered sign-boards, and emblems of their various trades gilt and varnished. At an early hour in the day the streets are all in commotion, and, amongst the novelties to an European eye, are the tribes of athletic half-clad porters, employed in the conveyance of every species of merchandise, whose noisy vociferations, and the throng and jostle which they occasion, create a bustle and confusion not inferior to that produced by the carts and carriages of other cities. The favourite vehicle is the sedan, or chair, borne upon men's shoulders. The bearers are exceedingly nimble, and possessed of powerful lungs; and their warnings and admonitions to the passers-by, the cries of the venders of various goods, the solicitations of beggars, and other clamorous sounds, are quite sufficient to banish all idea of quietude from these crowded avenues. The temples are extremely numerous; some of them are remarkable for their beauty, but the greater number are in a dilapidated state; all are open to every body, and many serve occasionally as theatres, gambling-houses, and taverns.

The temple of Honan, which rises on the bank of the river opposite to the factories, and at a short distance from them, is exceedingly handsome. Entering through a portico guarded by colossal figures cut out of granite, representing two famous Chinese warriors, the visitor is conducted into a spacious court, surrounded by very picturesque buildings, planted with fine trees, and adorned with numerous images of Bhood and his disciples, of all dimensions, some being colossal and others extremely small. This temple is well endowed, and supports a great number of priests, who, with the exception of a few offerings presented to the shrines, are left to the sole performance of religious worship, the Chinese troubling themselves very little about the care of their souls. Buddhism is not calculated to create any thing like enthusiasm on the part of its disciples; it inculcates an utter disregard to all the social duties, separates the parent from the child, the husband from the wife, and recommends a gloomy and sullen abstraction as the most acceptable act of devotion to a deity for ever wrapped up in solemn meditation.

The national indifference to religion may be partly attributed to the conduct of its ministers. The priesthood of Bhood has sunk into contempt in China, where its ranks are recruited from the lowest classes, men destitute of learning, and of notoriously profligate character. The temples which possess good revenues of their own are overcrowded with priests, and those belonging to others not so amply endowed are obliged to pick up a miserable subsistence from charity, often denied, and always grudgingly bestowed. Few are in these days distinguished for learning; their zeal for the honour of the god, and their devotion to his service, being chiefly displayed by utter seclusion from the affairs of this world, and a sort of misanthropic contempt of mankind; a mode of conduct which does not excite a very high degree of veneration amongst so lively a people as the Chinese, who in this respect differ widely from the more imaginative Hindoos, who are struck with admiration by the sacrifices made by religious ascetics, and load those who are capable of yielding them with little less than divine honours.

The Buddhist priesthood of China assume yellow robes during the period employed in religious worship, which consists of chanting, beating of gongs, counting rosaries, and performing the *ko-tow* before the gilded images of their god. In the immediate vicinity of the temple of Honan there are pigsties for the accommodation of several pigs, which are allowed to gorge until they die of suffocation from the accumulation of fat, though, before the attainment of this delectable condition, a few are sacrificed at the usual festival held in honour of the god. Thus, Buddhism in China, with its encouragement of infanticide, its ignorant and licentious priesthood, its brutal appendages, and its swinish feasts, appears under a hideous aspect, presenting one of the most fearful mockeries of religion which the world can afford.

The manufactures and trades of Canton are exceedingly numerous, but there is no machinery that can bear the slightest comparison with that of Europe, and in consequence no large manufacturing establishments under one superintendant are to be found. The Chinese have not yet learned the value of time, or the proper distribution of labour, and commercial speculators are still unacquainted with the best methods of employing capital. About seventeen thousand persons are engaged in Canton in weaving silk, which is a profitable occupation; and it is said that some of the females who devote their time to the finer kind of embroidery can earn from twenty to twenty-five dollars per month. Though this and other sources of emolument are open to them, the condition of women in China is extremely miserable; those belonging to the lower orders are, perhaps, the best off, since, notwithstanding their being made domestic drudges, they enjoy their liberty, and are of some importance to their husbands, while the women of a higher class, incapacitated by the distortion of their feet from any active exertion, are despised, and regarded as beings of an inferior order. The birth of a daughter is always the subject of regret in China, and in former times the luckless infant was cast upon one side, and left to take its chance for life during three days after its entrance into the world.

AURUNGZEBE'S TOMB,—ROZAH.

Rozah is a small town in the province of Aurungabad, and about fourteen miles from the city which gives its name to the district. It stands upon a highly elevated tract of table-land, the summit of a hill-pass between Dowlatabad and Ellora, and commands a very beautiful and extensive view. Aurungabad appears in the distance; and the bold abrupt conical mound, the pyramidal wonder of the scene, crowned with a bristling rampart, and deeply scarped at the base, the most singular of the hill-fortresses of India, forms a conspicuous object. Dowlatabad is only distant six miles and a half from Rozah, and from no point of view can it be seen to more advantage. The town is approached from a well-paved causeway, twenty feet wide: it is surrounded by a wall, constructed with great elegance and solidity, and contains numerous relics of its former wealth and magnificence; but the sculptured walls of the palaces of the Omrahs, who in the days of Moghul glory reared their proud pinnacles to heaven, are fast verging to the last stages of decay.

AURUNGZEBE'S TOMB, ROZAH.

AN OLD FORT AT MUTTRA.

Rozah being the royal burial-ground during the period in which Aurungabad formed the capital of Aurungzebe's dominions, its neighbourhood is thickly strewed with tombs of great and pious men. Probably, in the first instance, its boasting the mausoleums of several reputed saints may have occasioned a monarch, who either felt or feigned the strongest zeal for the cause of Mohamedism, to select it for the place of his own sepulture. The tomb of the last of the descendants of Timur Lung, who maintained the ancestral glory bequeathed to them by that mighty conqueror, rises within the same enclosure in which the remains of a Moslem saint are deposited. The mausoleum of Seid Zin Ul Abdeen eclipses in splendour that of the occupant of the hundred thrones of Hindoostan, and his memory is far more highly reverenced; Aurungzebe's tomb, though picturesque, has little claim to elegance or grandeur. The monarch's taste and liberality have been called in question by those who suppose it to have been his own work, but the usurper affected great plainness and simplicity in his own person: if, therefore, he was himself the founder of his monument, it was only in keeping with the character he desired to maintain; and if he left the care of his remains to his successors, we cannot be surprised by the scanty honours paid to them. Upon attaining the summit of his ambition, Aurungzebe rendered his dominion acceptable to the people whom he governed; but his public virtues were obscured by the atrocities of his private life, his filial impiety, and the cruel persecution of his more beloved brothers. Though enduring the monarch who ruled with wisdom and moderation, the vast multitude, readily yielding obedience to laws justly administered, detested the man; and, notwithstanding the reputation for sanctity which he strove to acquire, the emperor remains uncanonized; and while his relics are resigned to the care of a few of the most indigent of the priesthood, incense is burned and flowers are still strewed before the neighbouring shrines. The marble sarcophagus containing the ashes of the last of the conquering Moghuls, is covered with a paltry canopy of wood, which has now a very wretched and ruinous appearance; lamps are no longer lighted before it, and the utmost neglect is visible in every part. Some of the monarch's family repose in the same enclosure, but the whole is little worthy of a visit, except upon account of the unenviable greatness of the name which Aurungzebe has bequeathed to posterity.

AN OLD FORT AT MUTTRA.

There can be no question of the superior pleasure to be derived, in India, by those who in their travels are enabled to follow the course of the rivers, and to enjoy at ease the perpetual change of scenery which their banks afford. In many portions of the plains of Hindoostan there is a good deal of monotony, but the voyagers of the Ganges and the Jumna have their attention continually kept alive by a succession of landscapes of the highest interest. Emerging from a wide waste of waters, rendered more savage by a few islands of sand peering above them, where the huge alligator lies basking in the sun, or gigantic cranes watch for their prey, the boat suddenly passes some populous village, some romantic city, or some splendid temple, rising in solitary majesty amid encircling woods.

The lofty, dark, and frowning walls of the fort at Muttra, especially when seen against the red flush of an Eastern sunset, have a very imposing appearance from the river. In coming down with the current, it is reached very shortly after it is descried; but in toiling up against the stream, full leisure is permitted to gaze upon the massive bastions which have in former times successfully opposed the hostile projects of the surrounding chieftains. This castellated edifice stands upon the western bank of the Jumna, and was in former times a place of great strength: its appearance is still formidable, and its walls cover a large extent of ground, containing many buildings of various degrees of interest. Amongst the objects of curiosity to be found within the gates, are the remains of an observatory built by Rajah Jye Singh, a sovereign of Jeypore. The once beautiful and still striking relic of feudal power at Muttra has been, like many other castles and fortresses of British India, allowed to become the prey of time. The necessity, formerly so great, of furnishing every district with defences against the sudden attacks of numerous predatory hordes, no longer exists. Even previous to the fall of Bhurtpore, the garrison of the neighbouring cantonments sufficed to keep the most turbulent spirits in awe; and since that far-famed citadel has been stormed and taken, none of the native princes of India can venture to entertain a hope of recovering the power which has been wrested from them, in their quarrels with each other, by the strangers who rule the land.

Muttra is a stronghold of Hindoo superstition; previous to the early Mahomedan conquests it was a city of great sanctity and importance, reverenced as the birth-place of Krishna, the Hindoo Apollo. Its splendid temples and shrines, in which the idols were of pure gold, are supposed to have tempted Mahmood of Ghizni to invade the country. He carried off their treasures; and the immense value of the spoil with which he loaded his camels, inviting others to follow his example, the temples were soon plundered of all that he had either left or overlooked, and in these days not a vestige is to be found of the jewelled ornaments formerly so profusely lavished upon the idols of Hindostan. Mahmood, in the fulfilment of the duty enjoined to all true believers, overthrew the principal pagoda at Muttra; it was afterwards rebuilt by Rajah Beer Singh Deo, of Oorcha, who expended thirty-six lacs of rupees in the erection. Aurungzebe, a bigot not less zealous than his predecessor, destroyed the temple a second time, and constructed a mosque with the materials on its site, which may vie in splendour with those of Delhi and Agra. But the Moslem conquerors, though planting the crescent upon the prostrate ruins of heathen altars, could not succeed in rooting out, or even diminishing, the spirit of idolatry, or the worship of wood and stone,—which existed in its fullest extent at the period in which the city fell into the hands of the British government.

The Scindiah family had become possessed of Muttra towards the conclusion of the eighteenth century, the descendants of Aurungzebe being incapable of keeping together the vast empire which he had acquired. It surrendered without resistance in 1803 to Lord Lake, although it was then the head-quarters of General Perron, commandant of Scindiah's army, who had strengthened the fortifications, and put it into a position of defence. According to the policy which we have always pursued in our conquests in India, Lord Lake not only protected the persons and spared the property of the inhabitants, but also shewed respect for the prejudices of their religion. He commanded his troops to abstain from the slaughter of bullocks, and it is only lately that beef has been killed and eaten in the neighbourhood of this abode of the Brahmins. The Hindoo temples contained in the city are, as it may be supposed, very numerous; though inferior in point of size, and the grandeur of their design, to the places of Brahminical worship, which excite wonder in some other parts of India, they are finished with great elegance; and the architectural splendours of the Ghauts, with their accompanying pagodas, at Muttra, exceed in beauty the numerous superb landing-places which spread themselves on both sides of the Jumna, and are to be found adorning its wildest solitudes. The city is well built, after the Indian fashion; many of the houses are constructed with much solidity, the walls being massive and lofty, and embellished with richly carved ornaments in wood and stone: its principal distinction, however, consists in the the troops of monkeys with which the whole of its avenues swarm. These creatures are to be seen every where, and, as at Bindrabund, are said to know their own districts, none daring to intrude upon the quarters of their nearest neighbours. At both places, young European officers are frequently tempted to give a few rupees to the Brahmins, to provide a feast for the tribe under their immediate protection. The sight of the provision attracts many eyes, but, though wistfully regarding the good things spread out before the lawful owners, those living across the border, aware that they have no right to partake, keep at a respectful distance, and make no attempt to seize a share. Monkeys are reverenced by the Hindoos in consequence of one of their religious fables, in which Humaioon is said to have led an army of these animals to the assistance of their god Rama, when worsted in his conflicts with the great Ravanu. Paroquets, peacocks, pigeons, and Brahmanee bulls are nearly equally abundant, but, with the exception perhaps of the latter, not half so troublesome as the monkeys, which are considered a nuisance even by the Hindoos themselves. There is no possibility of keeping them out of any place which they choose to invade; they climb upon the tops of the houses, descend into the interior courts and gardens, perch upon the walls and door-posts, and assail the passengers below with missiles. Few persons have rambled through the streets of Muttra without having experienced this kind of annoyance from a race prone to every sort of mischief. To kill or maltreat these disagreeable neighbours would even now be attended with very serious consequences. Not many years ago, two young officers who fired at a monkey at Bindrabund, were drowned in the Jumna, in the vain attempt to escape from the rage of an exasperated multitude pursuing them to their destruction.

Muttra during a considerable period was a very important station to the British government, and, as long as the frontier was limited to its neighbourhood, it was garrisoned by a large brigade of troops. Since the occupation of Neemuch and Nusseerabad, and the vast extent of territory which we have acquired in remote districts, it has dwindled into insignificance. The troops have been greatly reduced in number, and the utmost quietude and tranquillity now reigns, though it is surrounded by a multitude of native chieftains, who may be supposed to be the least inclined, amid all the people of India, to submit to a government which precludes the hope of their regaining the despotic power over life and limb which they formerly exercised. The fort at Muttra. though no longer required for the purpose of defence, might still be rendered useful in some mercantile capacity; and we trust that the introduction of commercial speculations, will preserve this and similar edifices from the fate which must befall them, unless the progress of decay shall be speedily arrested.

RAMESWAR,—CAVES OF ELLORA

The view in the accompanying engraving represents the exterior of one of the excavations of Ellora, which, in consequence of the belief that some of the sculptures commemorate the nuptials of Ram and Seeta, has received the name of Rames war, or Rameswarra. It is one of the smallest of the range, the extreme length being ninety feet, and the breadth twenty-six feet six inches: opening from it, there is another chamber of the same character, and the whole is highly finished and beautifully designed. The figures in the interior are sculptured in compartments; they consist of many fine groups, and all, though more particularly that from which the name is derived, are considered admirable specimens of an early age of art. The pillars, also, which run along the front, are exquisitely carved, and their massive grandeur is in fine keeping with the almost awful sublimity of the scene. Less has been written about Ellora, and fewer excursions have been made by intellectual travellers to remains as magnificent and mysterious as the gigantic shrines of Egypt, than to any spot of equal celebrity upon the face of the earth. The desecration of their altars have rendered the natives indifferent to temples which manifest the noble and exalted ideas entertained by the founders, of the divinities to whom they were dedicated, but though long deserted, and disregarded by the worshippers of Bhood, and Brahma, the sanctity of these temples will survive the downfall of idolatry in India, their fame will spread to distant nations, and their splendours attract pilgrims from foreign lands, long after the whole fabric of Hindoo mythology shall be broken to pieces and overthrown. Even now, christian spectators regard the cave temples of Ellora with far greater reverence than that with which the descendants of the projectors of these mighty works survey the wondrous scene. Though surrounded by grotesque idols, the emblems and symbols of the most corrupt faith which has ever enchained the minds of intellectual beings, the vastness and loftiness of the design, the number and magnitude of these rock-hewn cathedrals, and the solemn grandeur of their effect, create a feeling of religious awe which cannot be repressed. The soul lifts itself up to the Deity, amid the dim and pillared aisles of these gigantic temples; nor is their exterior less inspiring, their porticoes and gateways seem to be the openings to another world: it is difficult to separate the workmanship of man from that of the Divine framer of the rocky hill; both appear to emanate from a power far superior to that which has piled stone upon stone together; and the most splendid architectural wonders of the world fade before the stupendous magnificence of the cave temples at Ellora.

RAMESWUR — CAVES OF ELLORA.

PULO PENANG.

PULO PENANG.

The island of Pulo Penang, or, as it is usually denominated, Prince of Wales' Island, is advantageously situated opposite to the Queda coast of the Malay peninsula. Standing at the entrance of the straits of Malacca, it forms a picturesque and beautiful object from the sea. A range of lofty mountains, whose irregularly towering summits afford a striking and majestic outline, first presents itself to view; and, as the voyagers approach, they are charmed by the neat and tasteful appearance of the houses which peep forth from shady groves, giving out all the spicy odours of an Indian isle.

The bay is edged with well-built bungalows, standing in the centre of luxuriant gardens; and the fort, projecting into the water, arrests the eye as it wanders over the adjacent town; while the scattered villas, luxuriant plantations, craggy hills, with the distant islands closing in the view, complete a panorama of no common degree of interest.

The island of Penang is about sixteen miles long and eight broad. It lies in latitude 5° 25′ north, and longitude 100° 19′ east, with the exception of two plains of inconsiderable length, on the eastern and western shore, the whole surface is hill, and, on account of the scantiness of the soil, little adapted to agricultural purposes. It is supposed that the mildness of the temperature, and the fertility of the earth, is produced by the evaporation occasioned by the woods, those portions of the island which have been cleared becoming less productive every year. But though the soil is not favourable to many kinds of culture, there is no appearance of sterility; the rich clothing of trees, the nutmegs, cloves, pepper, and golden fruits, which adorn Penang, surpassing those of the continent both in splendour and flavour, impress the casual visiter with extraordinary ideas of its fertility. To a stranger's eye, nature appears to put on her brightest and richest garb, the vegetation seems to be the most vigorous in the world; and all who touch upon the coast entertain this idea, since fruit and foliage continue in unfading splendour throughout the year. Pine-apples, especially, arrive at the highest degree of perfection; and although the mangosteen, the most celebrated of tropic fruits, does not grow upon the island, it is imported from the neighbouring scenes of its cultivation in such large quantities, as to afford an ample supply to all the inhabitants. Some estimate may be formed of the redundant growth of the plantain and pine-apple, by the specimens which appear in the sketch before us. Both have attained a gigantic size, and the beautiful pale-green feathering foliage of the former, a distinguishing feature of tropic scenery, renders it one of the most prominent and graceful ornaments of an Indian landscape.

The Chinese settlers in the neighbouring island of Singapore, convert the fibres of the leaves of the pine-apple into a peculiarly fine thread, from which fabrics of an exceedingly beautiful and delicate texture are made in China, whence the material is exported. It is thought that the preparation could be carried on with great advantage at Penang, where labour is extremely cheap, the process being simple, and a considerable portion fitted for the employment of women and children. The texture of this material very much resembles the flax of New Zealand, and though each fibre may be subdivided into threads so extremely delicate as to be scarcely perceptible, there is no want of strength, and the whole is so well adapted for the manufacture of linens and cambrics, that it will probably become a considerable article of commerce between the islands of the Eastern Archipelago and England.

The town of Penang is of some extent, and remarkable for its neatness, the bazaars especially being much better kept than those of Bengal. It is composed of wide straight streets, crossing at right angles, of a very respectable appearance, and tenanted by Chinese shopkeepers, a thriving thrifty race, who, wherever they settle, are certain of reaping the reward of their industry. The roads are excellent, and conduct the visiter to many scenes of romantic beauty. Those who are induced to make a pilgrimage to Penang in search of health, usually take up their residence on the hill overlooking the town, whence the accompanying view is taken. This eminence is studded with picturesque buildings, that to the right being the convalescent bungalow; while the government residence, with its flag-staff, appears upon the left: the town stretches out along the low point of land in the centre, and, opposite, the Queda shore closes the harbour, which is usually rendered animated by the ships of different nations.

The hill, though exempt from the sultriness of the neighbouring valleys, is subjected to mists and fogs, and cloudy visitations, which offer only a choice of evils. The climate of Penang would be very overpowering, were it not mitigated by the sea-breeze, but such is the cooling influence of these ocean gales, that many persons who cannot live in Bengal with all the alleviations afforded by punkahs, tatties, and other luxurious contrivances, require nothing but open doors and windows in those bungalows, which are slightly elevated, and look out upon the ocean; and every body who has enjoyed the sights and scenes afforded by glittering days and heavenly nights, in this enchanting region, must remember the sensations which they produced with the most intense pleasure.

The military duties of Penang are performed by a sepoy regiment belonging to the Bengal army, volunteering for the service; the native troops never being sent on board ship, excepting by their own free choice. Their European officers, the governor and his dependants, with a few others, form the only portion of the highest class of the community not wholly mercantile. The golden dreams, formerly cherished, are speedily vanishing from the anxious eyes of those who are engaged in commercial speculations, the neighbouring settlement at Singapore having allured nearly all the trade from Penang; yet, notwithstanding the disappointment of their expectations, the merchants are still numerous, clinging to the hope of better times, which, perhaps, were they to attend very diligently to some of the hitherto neglected products of the island, would be nearer at hand than is now imagined. Penang is at present what Calcutta used to be, a place of the most boundless hospitality, a characteristic which disappears before an extending population; the society being very limited, the arrival of every stranger is immediately known, and he is made welcome at every table without much examination of his title to an introduction to the best houses. As a settled residence, perhaps, Penang, notwithstanding its social meetings, and the picturesque beauty that surrounds it, would become wearisome; but, for a casual abode, there are few places which can afford a higher degree of satisfaction to those who delight in viewing the loveliest productions of nature. The flowers and the birds of the beautiful islands of these Indian seas, are infinitely more brilliant than their continental namesakes; here are to be found the loories which gleam like a constellation of gems, and those superb crested cockatoos, of snowy white, which, on expanding their soft thick plumage, display the orange tinge beneath, changing at once from silver to gold. The palm-tree rises to the height of a hundred and thirty feet, the creepers trail their large and lustrous flowers along thickets perfumed with spices, and the pitcher, and other curious plants, mingle with fern lichens and fungi, glowing with every colour of the rainbow. Amongst the numerous vegetable productions worthy of note at Penang, is the elastic-gum vine, or caoutchouc tree, *(urce elastica,)* from which the substance called Indian rubber is produced. It is a parasitical plant, with a stem nearly round, and about three or four inches in diameter, having an ash-coloured bark. It will creep along the ground sometimes to the distance of five hundred feet, putting out roots at short intervals, but, upon coming to a tree, it climbs up the trunk, and twines itself around the very highest branches. The juice is obtained by bleeding the vine, or by cutting it in pieces when the plant has become old; the latter is the usual method of treatment, and it will then yield nearly two-thirds of its own weight. The neighbouring ocean produces a white sea-weed, called Agar-agar, which is exported in large quantities to China; it is remarkably succulent, and is formed into a strong jelly or glue, in which state it is used for various purposes: tasteless in itself, when mixed with sugar, lime-juice, and rose water, it affords a dainty and ornamental appendage to a dinner table, but it is principally employed as a size, or cement, for stiffening linens, preparing paper, &c.

The sail from Penang to Singapore presents the loveliest succession of island scenery which old ocean can produce; the sea is actually studded with tracts of fairy land, glittering like emeralds in the golden sun, where the waving trees dip their long branches into the water, where the smooth sands are covered with shells sparkling with all the hues of the prism, and where birds of orient plumage skim over the surface of the silver sea, or glance in and out from groves laden with the richest foliage of fruit and flower. These beautiful combinations of wood and valley, dazzling ocean and shaded landscape, whether lighted up by a glorious sun, fading in the mysterious veil of twilight, illumined by a cloudless moon, or softly revealed by the faint radiance of the stars, afford endless gratification to the rapt spectator who possesses a soul to appreciate the tender sublimity of the scene. As the vessel glides along, the interest is kept up by constant changes. The ocean, land-locked on every side, maintains an unruffled calmness; a gentle ripple is alone perceptible during the strongest winds, but now it spreads into a broad expanse, and now winds through the narrowest inlets. Squalls which threaten to drive vessels under water, have very little effect upon the smooth unagitated bosom of the deep, which, amid these flowery labyrinths, retains its placidity during the brief dominion of the summer tempests.

JERDAIR.

The small and obscure village of Jerdair stands upon a mountain slope in the province of Gurwall, a tract of country extending on the north-west to the banks of the Sutledj, on the north-east to the summit of the Himalaya, and bounded on the east and south by the British province of Delhi. It is an exceedingly hilly or rather mountainous tract, difficult of cultivation; yet parts of it are particularly fertile, and, though now thinly peopled, it bears the remains of mighty works, the undertakings of former possessors of the soil. The sides of many of the hills exhibit a succession of terraces of very solid construction; and upon the surfaces thus produced, the water necessary for the cultivation of rice is retained. Several branches of the Ganges flow through the valleys of this highly picturesque country, which is regarded with peculiar veneration by the people of Hindoostan, in consequence of its containing the holy ground from which the infant waters of the true Ganges issue into open light. Formerly this province comprehended all the territory extending to Hurdwar, and stretched eastward to the borders of Nepal, but it is now restricted within much narrower limits, and forms one of the British dependencies, under the perchance nominal rule of a native rajah, who is indebted for the restoration of his dominions to our arms, and who is protected by soldiers in our service.

Notwithstanding its extreme elevation, the climate of Gurwall, owing to its south-western aspect, is very mild; and though the site of the village of Jerdair presents a black and barren waste, the greater portion of this province is finely and richly clothed with trees. In many places, the productions of the temperate and the torrid zones meet and mingle: the tiger makes his lair upon the confines of eternal snow; and the elephant is enabled to endure the severity of the climate, by a provision of nature unknown to animals of his species, the natives of warmer latitudes,—a shaggy covering of hair. The bases of the immense ranges of these mountain districts are spread with thick forests, exhibiting all the redundant vegetation of a tropic clime; upon ascending, this character continues for a short distance, but soon the rhododendron makes its appearance amongst the bushes, and a stray daisy is found enamelling the grass; a little higher, the oak and the pine usurp the places of the teak and the neem; the giant creepers become exhausted, and give way to ferns, mosses, and lichens; the places of the wild castor, the oleanders, and other shrubs, are supplied by raspberries, barberries, dog-roses, thorns, and brambles, the holly shews its variegated leaf, and wild pears put forth their snowy blossoms; nettles and thistles spring up on every side—and the whole assumes the aspect of the tangled wastes of Europe. Occasionally the appearance of some decidedly Asiatic production reminds the English traveller that he is in a distant quarter of the globe; but at the elevation of three thousand feet, few of this character are to be seen. Higher up the forest is almost wholly pine, some of which attain to an enormous size. As the cold increases, the trees become fewer, stunted in their growth, and occur in scattered groups;

JERDAIR, — A HILL VILLAGE, — GURWALL.

ENTRANCE TO THE CAVE OF ELEPHANTA.

Oriental landscape. Pens and pencils, however, have lately been very briskly at work; the voyage to India is now so much shortened, that gentlemen be' nging to the civil or military establishment can find time to travel through many parts of Europe during the period of their furlough, and have thus an opportunity of acquiring a taste for the picturesque, and the power of making comparisons between the most celebrated places of the western world, and the hitherto little regarded scenery of India. Details of tiger hunts and curried soups, shawls, dragon china, and gold bangles, have been superseded by, or intermixed with animated descriptions of temple and tower, lake and bowery grove; and though there are still many excellent persons who cast anchor in the harbour of Bombay without having the slightest desire to visit any thing but the well-spread tables of the inhabitants of the seat of government, or, if joining a pic-nic party to Elephanta, think much more of cooling the claret than of the examination of the caves,—the greater number are capable of appreciating the surrounding beauties of nature and art; those who do not commit their ideas to paper, assisting in creating and disseminating a taste for the study of Indian history and antiquities.

Elephanta is the name given to an island about six miles in circumference, which lies at nearly the same distance from the usual place of anchorage for vessels of large burden at Bombay, and four or five from the Mahratta shore. The appellation was conferred upon it by the Portuguese, in consequence of a colossal figure of an elephant carved out of the solid rock, which formed a striking object on the south side of the island, but which is now almost beyond the reach of restoration; the head and neck severed themselves from the body in 1814, and the trunk has since almost buried itself in the earth. The carving of this effigy was of the rudest description, and it never had any thing to recommend it except its gigantic dimensions. The natives of Bombay have not adopted the new appellation, but still continue to call the island by its ancient name, Gare-poori, the Place of Caves. The visiters on landing are conducted up a steep and narrow pathway, not practicable for any conveyance, excepting a chair or palanquin; it winds through very interesting scenery, the hill being well wooded, and the road sometimes stretching along the brink of a precipice, and at others serpentining through rich groves, where the *gloriosa superba* spreads its clustering flowers, and where, from other luxuriant creepers, those red berries are culled, which both in India and England are strung in necklaces. The prospects obtained of the harbour, the opposite shore of Salsette, and of the northern part of the island, are very bold and striking. From the cave itself, glimpses may be caught between the interstices of the surrounding trees, of the distant ghauts, and the upper parts of the beautiful bay, which is broken into innumerable ridges, and thickly covered with luxuriant foliage, amongst which the splendid coronals of the tara palm are the most conspicuous: while the whole affords one of the grandest displays of tropical forest scenery, with its bright and never-fading verdure, its gigantic leaves, and brilliant blossoms, which is to be found along this interesting coast.

About two-thirds up the ascent of the hill, a beautiful platform leads to the entrance of the grand cave, roofed in by the wood-crowned mountain, and presenting through its multiplicity of pillars a beautiful perspective along cathedral-like aisles, of vast dimensions.

the birch gradually diminishes to a dwarf, and soon afterwards the only vegetation consists of mosses and lichens, hardy tribes, existing upon the very verge of eternal snow.*

Serinagur was formerly the capital of Gurwall, but on the return of its sovereign, who had sought a retreat from the invasion of the Ghorkas in the British territories, and took no part in its restoration, this city being comprised in the ceded portion of the district, the village of Barahaut became a place of importance, from being selected for the seat of the native government. The inhabitants of Gurwall are termed Khayasa, and all boast their descent from Rajpoots of the highest caste, and are therefore exceedingly scrupulous in their eating, and in their regard for the sacred cow. They will not sell one of these animals, excepting upon an assurance that the purchaser will neither kill it himself, nor suffer it to be killed by another; their prejudices prevent them from keeping poultry, and travellers must bring sheep with them, or subsist upon fish and game. Both are exceedingly abundant, and the former so plentiful as to be easily caught by the hand; but the precipitous nature of the country renders the toil of the sportsman very severe, as birds drop at an immense distance from the place whence they are shot, and are frequently lost in impenetrable ravines.

Many of the bursts of mountain scenery which occur as the footpaths wind round some projecting point are magnificently sublime, the high ledges of the rock are the haunt of the chamois, and eagles have their eyries on the hoary peaks. These and the neighbouring provinces are remarkable for a peculiar breed of ponies, called ghoouts, rough, stunted, and shaggy, but exceedingly sure-footed, and well adapted to carry a traveller in safety along the dizzy verge of narrow pathways, which look down upon some dreadful abyss.

ENTRANCE TO THE CAVE OF ELEPHANTA.

The harbour of Bombay is now acknowledged to be one of the most beautiful anchoring grounds in the world, little if at all inferior to the far-famed bay of Naples, and claiming the admiration of those who visit it, not more for the wonderful monuments of art which its islands contain, than for the picturesque grandeur of its scenery. There can be no greater proof of the progress of taste, and the spread of intellect, than that afforded by the newly excited curiosity which has been awakened by the descriptions given in modern tours and journals, of the beauties of British India. We can scarcely believe, that from the period in which the island of Bombay was ceded to England by the Portuguese, on the marriage of Charles II. with their Infanta, it should have been the resort of vast numbers of Englishmen of liberal education, who were quite equal to the task of transmitting to their brethren at home a just description of the splendid scenery of the land of their adoption. But the union of the sword and the quill, the ledger and the diary, was not thought of, or rarely occurred, in those times; and the few learned men who wrote about India, confined themselves for the most part to antiquarian researches, which, however valuable to the scholar or to the student in search of solid information, did nothing to render the subject popular, or to convey an idea of the extraordinary beauties of the

* Views of this interesting region are now in preparation by the Publishers, from sketches on the spot, by Lieut. White; re-drawn by Messrs. Turner, Prout, Bentley, Melville, Allom, Purser, &c. &c.

ASSAR MAHAL,—BEEJAPORE.

The island of Elephanta is not inhabited; and the caves, like those of Ellora, are desecrated, no longer inspiring the Hindoo with any religious feeling; but they are still haunted by a few poor Brahmins; and the parties who come over to explore their wonders have usually sufficient respect to the prejudices of these persons, not to introduce beef at the banquet spread under the once sacred roof. The view given in the plate represents the front, or principal entrance, but there are two others of correspondent beauty, all hewn out of a stone, resembling porphyry; the interior of the cave is rather gloomy, and torches are necessary for the examination of the sculptures with which it is profusely carved. One of the most celebrated of these ornaments, the gigantic Triad bust, has been described in a former page of this work, the remainder for the most part are also Brahminical; but two images of Bhood have intruded themselves amongst this strange company, and have suffered more severely than their adversaries from the holy animosity of the Portuguese.

ASSER MAHAL, BEEJAPORE.

The accompanying plate affords a representation of one of the numerous palaces now in the last stage of ruin, which embellished the once flourishing capital of Beejapore: it stands upon the edge of a broad moat, which encircles the citadel in the central quarter of the city, and a part wherein the progress of decay has been more rapid and extensive than in almost any one of the desolate avenues of this deserted place. We learn, from scattered notices in Ferishta's history, and from other sources, that the riches of the chiefs and omrahs of the Adil Shah monarchs of Beejapore were not inferior to the displays made in any other Mohammedan kingdom of India; the concourse of elephants, in particular, those imposing adjuncts of barbaric show, was very great. We hear of studs consisting of three hundred of these animals; and in no place could they be shewn to more advantage, or amid more splendid accompaniments, than the lofty towers, gigantic domes, and soaring pinnacles of Beejapore.

This place was distinguished for its feasts and festivals, more especially for the celebration of the Mohurrum, which the great majority of the inhabitants, being Sheeas, kept with the greatest degree of solemnity and splendour. Yusuf Adil Shah, the founder of the kingdom, set an example of toleration, which was almost invariably followed by his successors. Inquiring of Mowlana Gheias-ood-Deen, a celebrated Persian Moollah, who had obtained a high reputation both for his learning and talents, and the purity of his life, which was the best of all the numerous sects of Islam; that devout person replied, "Suppose a great monarch to be seated in a palace with many gates leading to it, and through whichever you enter you see the king, and can obtain admission to his presence—your business is with the prince, and not with those at the gate." Some of Yusuf's followers, being Soonees, were inclined to withdraw when they saw that their master had adopted the religious opinions of their adversaries, but he detained them in his service by a promise of the free exercise of their faith; yet, notwithstanding this indulgence, so great was their animosity against the rival sect, that the king was obliged to watch narrowly over the chiefs of the Soony persuasion, who, encouraged by the determined hostility of other Mohammedan nobles established in the Deccan, could with difficulty be kept to their allegiance.

The annals of Beejapore contain some very curious instances of the political influence and the bold interference of women in affairs of state; for, notwithstanding the jealous exclusion of the Mohammedans of females from any part of the government, and the little weight which they permitted them to have in society, they contrived to take a very active part in the intrigues and revolutions of the court. The queen-mother saved her son Ismael Adil Shah from the usurpation of the regent Kumal Khan, to whose care the administration of the affairs of the kingdom had been entrusted during the minority of the young prince: the method taken was that of assassination, and she adroitly contrived to make an old woman, who had been placed as a spy over her, and who was devoted to the regent's interest, one of the principal, though unconscious, agents. The design, though successful as far as the despatch of Kumal Khan was concerned, had been nearly frustrated by the spirited measures taken by the mother of the regent, who concealed her son's death, brought the body out, dressed, and supported upon pillows, at an open balcony of the palace, to receive the homage of the nobles, and advised her grandson to repair instantly to the royal residence, and seize the person of the young king. The queen-mother, imagining from this movement that Kumal Khan had escaped the dagger which had been aimed at his heart, would have temporized, had not Dilshad Agha, the young monarch's foster-aunt, another high-souled and talented woman, come forward with her counsel. She told her auditors, that, in such a crisis, valour and fortitude would be of more avail than submission; ordered the palace gates to be shut; sent to the foreigners in her retinue, who had lately accompanied her from Persia, to inform them of the danger to which their sovereign, who was their countryman, was exposed from the ambition of Kumal Khan; stated that the palace was surrounded by the usurper's forces, who were advancing to put the king and all the royal family to death; and adjured them, if they were men, not to heed the superiority of numbers which the enemy could bring against them, but to stand up valorously for their prince, and overthrow the traitor, who, by the Divine blessing, would be punished for ingratitude, accursed in the eyes of God and man. The foreign guards instantly drew their weapons in defence of their young sovereign, and the queen-mother, together with Dilshad Agha, assumed men's attire, and appeared upon the walls clad in mail, and armed with bows and arrows, but still wearing their veils. The boy king, Ismael Adil Shah, accompanied them, attended by a Turkey female named Moortufa, who held the yellow umbrella, the emblem of sovereignty assumed by his father, over his head. An animated conflict commenced, but, though the females fought with ardour, their little party must soon have been cut to pieces, had not Dilshad Agha, with the skill of an experienced general, despatched messengers over the walls to all the Toorks resident in the city, and assisted those who attended the summons to scale the terraces by means of ropes. The outer gate was forced, but Dilshad Agha gallantly repulsed the besiegers; and the young king, perceiving that Jufdar Khan, the regent's son, had crouched down to avoid a flight of arrows by which he had been wounded, rolled a heavy stone upon his adversary's body, and victory soon afterwards declared in his favour.

RUINS ON THE SITE OF OLD DELHI.

RUINS OF OLD DELHI.

There is no adjunct which so completely devastates the neighbourhood of ruins, as sand. When vegetation has flung its graceful drapery over broken walls and prostrate towers, the mind becomes reconciled to the decay of man's most ostentatious work, but the effect of sand is to deepen every horror, to increase the dreariness of the waste, and to add the curse of sterility to the ravages of time; yet is there still something sublime in the utter desolation it produces. From the nature of the greater portion of the province of Delhi, it required the most strenuous efforts on the part of the inhabitants to counteract the progress of aridity; the deposites of the Jumna, unlike the fertilizing mud of the Ganges, consisting of washed and unproductive sand, while its waters are so strongly impregnated with carbonate of soda, that they prevent spontaneous vegetation, and destroy the labours of the cultivator wherever they are suffered to overflow. These desolating agents are not derived from the mountains whence the Jumna has its birth, but are taken up in the wide plain above the city of Delhi. The savage horror which now characterizes a scene once glowing with all the beauty which the luxuriance of a tropic soil and a tropic climate can bestow, has occasioned modern travellers to doubt the tales told of the former splendour of the imperial residence. M. Jacquemont, from whom we might have expected more solid information, calls the author of Lalla Rookh a perfumer and a liar, because he has described gardens of roses where some of the coarsest weeds refuse to grow; but we are not to judge of the aspect of Old Delhi, under its founders, by its present appearance. Had the troubles of this portion of Hindoostan, which lasted during the greater portion of a century, continued for a century longer, (which, but for the subjugation of the Mahratta power, they would have done,) the Jumna, unrestricted in its wanderings, would have gradually laid the whole of the Dooab waste, carrying the drifting sand to the banks of the Ganges, and changing from a rapid river to one vast and melancholy jheel. Even the ruins which now tell the tale of former glory, must have been swept away, and visitors, refusing to credit any thing which they do not see, might have doubted the existence of the tombs and palaces, as well as of the roses which flourished beneath their walls.

Old Delhi, founded upon the site of the ancient Hindoo city of Indraput, by the Afghan invaders of Hindoostan, was ruined and laid waste by other Moslem conquerors. The followers of Timur avenged upon the descendants of Gengis Khan, the excesses which he and his fellow-victors had committed. Delhi was taken and sacked, its splendid avenues presented one wide scene of conflagrations and massacre, and it never afterwards recovered its original splendour. After the withdrawal of Timur, who was called away from his triumphs in Hindoostan, to repel the aggression of the Turkish emperor, Bajazet, the sceptre of India was swayed by weak hands, until the accession of Baber, whose reign was too short to enable him to repair all the mischief which had occurred under the misrule of his predecessors. Shere Shah, who wrested the throne from the son of this prince, though anxiously attentive to the improvement of the country, did not live to complete all his designs; the reign of Humaioon, who succeeded, was of very brief duration, and Acbar fixed the capital of his empire at Agra. When Shah Jehan ascended the throne of the Moghuls, Delhi exhibited only a miserable remnant of its former greatness; and, perhaps despairing of its restoration, he left it to its fate, and constructed the new city, which now has nearly shared the melancholy destiny of its predecessor. Many of the gardens which he planted have disappeared, but enough remain to convince those who desire to make themselves acquainted with the real facts of the case, to show that care and cultivation are alone necessary to convert this sterile wilderness into a blooming paradise. There is great difficulty in giving a name to some of the most perfect edifices which rear their lofty domes amongst the crumbling heaps laid prostrate by the hand of time. We have no authentic record to refer to, and the native Cicerones are not to be depended upon for the correctness of their accounts. The massive grandeur of the Pytan and Afghan architects it is impossible to mistake; many of the structures, reared by these splendid people, are still remarkable for their solidity; and nothing short of the wanton ravages of man, aided by the hostility of nature, would have caused so great a devastation, even throughout the lengthened period in which this magnificent city has been wholly abandoned to evil influences.

Old Delhi owed the greater portion of its most interesting edifices to Firoze Shah, who emploved a reign, of thirty-nine years, more than ordinarily exempt from the troubles and disturbances which have characterised empire in the East, almost entirely in the erection of public buildings. His plans were made upon the grandest scale; and the extent and durability of his works, which were not more remarkable for their gigantic dimensions than for the exquisite delicacy and beauty of their finish, to this day exite the wonder and admiration of the pilgrim who visits the scene of his labours. It was Firoze Shah who constructed the grand canal which brought fertility to this now neglected portion of the province. Soon after his decease, the Mahratta power, which has threatened to reduce the whole of India to a desert, began to be felt: amid all the struggles which succeeded, this power increased, until the necessity of seeking refuge within the walls of New Delhi from the lawless horde who tyrannized over the descendants of Aurungzebe, occasioned the total abandonment of the old city.

SINGHAM MAHAL,—TORWAY.

The remains of a royal palace, built by the former sovereigns of Bejapore, at a village called Torway, about five miles from the great western gate of the city, which has been so often referred to in the present work, are represented in the accompanying plate. This place also possesses the ruins of a mosque; and the fragments of other buildings, scattered around, shew that in former times it was a favourite retreat of royalty. The road from Poonah to Bejapore runs through Torway, and from several points magnificent views of the lonely capital of a once flourishing state present themselves. Here, as from all other places which command a prospect of the city, the majestic dome of Mahmood Shah arrests the eye, as it rises in solemn grandeur above the clustering towers and pinnacles of the surrounding buildings; and here the extreme desolation of the country, its scanty cultivation,

SINGHAM MAHAL, TORWAY,—BEJAPORE.

and the fewness of its inhabitants, impress the mind with the most melancholy feelings. Never perhaps could the visitor, who has followed at a distance the devastating progress of Mahratta conquest, see more striking proofs of the misery to which the dominion of that power has doomed every portion of the land submitting to its sway.

Delighting in a roving existence, preferring the uncertain shelter of a camp to the comfortable abodes of cities, the Mahrattas cared nothing for fine buildings, and the pomp of architecture was lavished upon them in vain. Indifferent to human suffering from long acquaintance with sights and scenes of wo, these people will see whole multitudes perishing by the wasting tortures of famine and disease, unmoved and untouched by any desire to administer to the comfort of their fellow-creatures. They are wanderers by choice, and the present moment alone occupies their attention or their thoughts; totally indifferent to the comforts of domestic life, they can be easily led to disregard its decencies. The greater number are content with the most miserable species of accommodation: a tent or *pal*, consisting merely of a blanket or piece of coarse cloth, stretched over a bamboo, placed upon the forked summits of two sticks driven into the ground, suffices for the habitations of the poorer classes, the rich indulge in two or three folds of cloth; the tent is closed at the extreme end, and furnished with a curtain in front, but it is utterly destitute of those conveniences which persons belonging to civilized communities class amongst the necessaries of life. In cold or wet weather, a group of Mahrattas may be seen huddling round a fire, smoking, or stupifying their faculties by the cheap ardent spirit of the country, which, unlike other inhabitants of India, they drink openly, without scruple or shame. Men and animals are crowded into a confined space; each consults his own peculiar comfort alone; and the want of systematic arrangements, and of all consideration for the public weal, produces individual suffering and distress, which is regarded with the most callous indifference.

As Hindoos, the Mahrattas are any thing but orthodox; the various castes composing the second class, permit themselves a very wide latitude in the article of food; they will eat any kind of flesh, excepting beef, whenever it comes in their way; they do not reject fowls or onions, which are considered sacred by other Hindoos: but their offences in this way are limited by their poverty, which compels them to subsist chiefly upon vegetable diet of the coarsest kind. They are a warlike people, priding themselves more upon their arms than upon the elegances of dress; the chiefs affect a degree of simplicity which amounts to meanness, and the lower orders are slovenly and squalid in their appearance. They seem to be as utterly devoid of public attachment as of the domestic affections, serving as mercenaries under any commander; constantly engaged in mutinies, the subject of their discontent being always the arrear of pay, and going one day over to the enemy, and returning the next; deceived by a few hollow promises, which experience might tell them are never kept. How so disorderly a race of people, and such a despotic yet temporizing government, could hold together, appears to be miraculous; but in despite of every sort of mal-administration, and of the horrors and aversion with which the atrocities committed by Mahratta victors inspired the people whom they conquered, the power of these hordes increased to such a fearful extent, that at one time it threatened the subversion of the whole peninsula.

Wherever the Moslems extended their dominion, they introduced new arts and new luxuries. In pulling down the temples of the heathens, they never failed to erect mosques of equal or superior magnificence in their stead; they converted waste places into cities, and left almost imperishable marks of their glory wherever they planted the standard of the prophet. The Mahrattas, on the contrary, passed like a pestilence over the land, blighting and destroying all that came within their baleful influence, and converting the fairest possessions into a desert. Bejapore perhaps has suffered less than any city which has been submitted to their tender mercies; they have set apart a portion of its revenues to the support of the attendants of its tombs and mosques; but still it bears very strongly the impress of Mahratta sway, and there is but too much reason to believe that the injuries which it has sustained are now beyond a remedy. The wasted plains of the Deccan will doubtless again be gladdened by the song of the reaper, its towns and villages will become populous, but the splendour of its architecture, if once lost, can never, we fear, be recovered

BENARES.

The annexed view is taken from the upper part of the city of Benares, looking down the Ganges; and it affords a lively idea of the splendid panorama which this celebrated place presents to those who have an opportunity of seeing it from the river. The minarets of Aurungzebe's mosque, at once the pride and shame of the holy city, appear in the distance; and the foreground is occupied by one of those stately but fortress-like mansions which are so commonly to be found all over India. There are a great many habitations equally large, and of equally solid construction, in Benares; they occupy an extensive portion of ground, each comprehending several quadrangles, or courts; and, considering the great bulk of the population, which is estimated at about 630,000 souls, and the comparatively narrow limits of the city, it is surprising that so much space could be permitted to one family, even though the persons composing it, and their retainers, might be exceedingly numerous. The seclusion so much affected by Asiatics in their domestic residences, is completely attained by the mode of building represented in the plate; where the walls are so high, and the towers so strong, the females may be indulged with something more than the few yards of sky to which the prospects of the greater portion of Hindostanee women of rank are limited. In some places, however, even the high terraces and elevated turrets running along the exterior surface of the walls, are the exclusive monopoly of the men, who may be seen in an evening enjoying the dewy air in these pleasant places, while their wives and daughters are fain to be content with some narrow confined court-yard below. The love of flowers, common to all the females of Hindoostan, must be an instinct rather than a taste: many never see them before they have been gathered.

They have no idea of water, except that which can be obtained from looking at it in a basin or jug, and it is scarcely possible to imagine the gross state of ignorance the jealousy of man has doomed beings as intellectual as himself. With some, the system works well; they are quiet under the tyranny, fancying, because it is only the lower orders of their sex who are indulged with liberty, that to be enslaved is to enjoy dignity, exclusive, and therefore

BENARES.

to be prized: others, more lively and intelligent, are possessed with an insatiable curiosity to acquire information respecting things which they are not permitted to see; they are continually tormenting those about them with questions, puerile, of course, since infants in European countries have better opportunities of obtaining knowledge; and, for want of more noble employment for the mind, they are apt to become harsh and tyrannical, many being known to exercise the greatest cruelty over their dependants. That instances of barbarity, practised by women reduced to so degraded a state, are not more frequent, is a strong argument in favour of the natural amiability of the sex in Hindoostan: it is not easy even for a European female to obtain access to the best society of natives of her own sex; but when such opportunities have occurred, the observations made have been highly favourable to the intellectual endowment of a class who have to struggle with so many disadvantages. Though few can read, they all speak correctly; and it is said that even the women-servants who have been brought up in the zenanas belonging to persons of rank, express themselves in very superior language to those who are employed in attendance upon European ladies. The Hindoostan females are frequently very expert at the needle, although that kind of employment does not belong exclusively to women. Men do not think it disgraceful to earn their subsistence by embroidery, and at Benares they may be seen sitting in open shops busily employed in flowering muslins: mending shawls is also a lucrative occupation; and many of their operatives are so expert as to make the worn-out portions which they have restored, so exactly resemble the rest of the web, as to defy the strictest examination. Shawls, considerably the worse for wear, are thus frequently sold for new ones at Benares; and it is not until they drop to pieces, that the purchaser discovers how much he has been deceived in his bargain.

Benares is famous for several manufactures. The striped washing silks which are worn there, are much in request for female garments: there are also gauzes of various kinds, and every description of gold and silver tissue and brocade; the last is called kincob, and is most frequently sold in the scales, fetching its own weight in gold, the silk with which it is intermixed paying for the workmanship. The Benares turbans are exceedingly splendid; some are formed of scarfs of gold or silver tissue, with rich bordered ends, and others are of velvet, so exquisitely wrought with the needle, as to look like a constellation of jewels. Besides these, and other native productions, Benares is one of the great marts of the riches of the East. Diamonds, pearls, and other precious gems, are brought from all parts of Asia, together with shawls, spices, gums, dyes, and perfumes. It is, perhaps, only here, and at a few other places, that the finest products of the looms of Dacca are procurable. Hindoostanee females of rank delight in attiring themselves in a drapery of a texture so thin and transparent, as scarcely to be visible except when folded many times together. This is called night-dew, and it is said that a certain monarch objecting to the indecency of his daughter's dress, was told that she had clothed herself in several hundred yards of muslin. This delicate article is very expensive, and in all probability never found its way into European markets.

The extraordinary influence which the British government has obtained in India, can in no place be more strongly displayed than in Benares, where the Brahmins were formerly lords of the ascendant, and might commit any act they pleased with perfect impunity: for the Mohammedans, though leaving a proud emblem of their triumph in the mosque, so often mentioned, did not make any permanent conquests in the immediate neighbourhood of the holy city. The privileges of a Brahmin are not recognized by the law of the British courts of judicature: if a murder be proved against him, he must suffer for the crime; and though all suicides cannot be prevented, they are far less frequent than heretofore. The curious custom of sitting dhurna, formerly so common amongst Hindoos, is not practised to so great an extent at Benares as in many other parts of India, where debts have been recovered, and grievances redressed, by the most extraordinary means which the weak ever devised against the strong. The oppressed party, either singly or in numbers, clothed in mourning attire, with ashes on the head, sit down in some convenient spot, refusing to eat or to sleep, until they shall obtain justice. The enemy, thus assailed, is compelled by the prejudices of his religion, if a Hindoo, to abstain from food also, until he can come to a compromise; the blood of the person dying under this strange infliction being upon his head. Even Christians, whose consciences have not been so tender upon the subject, have felt themselves awkwardly placed when the dhurna has been performing at their doors, especially at Benares, where, upon one occasion, nearly the whole population assumed the attitude of mourning, sitting exposed to the weather, and to the danger of starving, to procure the repeal of an obnoxious tax. The ghauts of Benares at another time exhibited the same strange and awful spectacle, upon the desecration of the sacred well by the blood of a cow killed by a Mussulman party: but such sights are becoming very rare; and, notwithstanding the superstition which now prevails in the lotus of the world, the learning for which it has been so highly celebrated will, no doubt, take a new direction, and lead, if not immediately to the establishment of Christianity, to a better form of religion, more nearly approaching to that pure deism of which the Brahminical worship is a corruption.

KYLAS—CAVES OF ELLORA.

The front entrance of Kylas, the heaven of Siva, one of the central excavations of the hill of Ellora, represented in the accompanying plate, from the want of uniformity of design, is less beautiful than many of the façades which have been sculptured in this noble range. But though deficient in exterior elegance, the cave of Kylas, of which the part exhibited in the engraving is merely an outwork, is perhaps the most splendid of any that Ellora can boast; and it is only necessary to refer to a former portion of this work, to bear out the assertion. The top of the pagoda, which stands insulated in the centre of a cleared area of considerable magnitude, and which is ornamented by several colossal statues, appears above the wall connecting the gateway and the chamber over it with the scarp of the rock. The summit of one of the obelisks is likewise to be seen, together with the hill which rises, though not to any great elevation, above.

FRONT VIEW OF THE KYLAS. CAVES OF ELLORA.

The height of this outer gateway is fourteen feet, and it leads into a passage having apartments on either side, fifteen feet by nine. The sculptures on the outside are partly Buddhist and partly Brahminican, and over the door is the Nagara Khana, or Music-room, the floor of which forms the roof of a passage leading from the entrance into the excavated area within. Notwithstanding the introduction of Buddhist emblems, the Kylas belongs to the Brahmins, being evidently, with those which occupy its immediate vicinity in the central range of the hill, dedicated to Siva, whose sacred bull occupies a conspicuous place in the interior. The antiquity of the Buddhist religion over that introduced by the Brahmins has been strongly insisted upon by many of the learned; but the greater number contend that the disciples of Bhood were the reformers of the wild creed, which converted attributes into deities in such multitudes, as to produce a perfect mob in its Olympus. Though having its origin in Hindoostan, Bhuddism is no longer to be found in the place of its birth; but its followers succeeded in spreading their creed over the greater part of Asia, where it still prevails, though in a very corrupted state. The four southern excavations of Ellora are pronounced to be Bhuddist; while those upon the northern side are more doubtful, being by many of the learned attributed to the Jains, who, however, can scarcely be said to follow a distinct religion, their images being the same as those to which the Buddhists pay homage, and their reverence for persons yielding themselves up to religious abstraction being equally profound. Though the Buddhists have been expelled from India, two sects of Jains still remain, who are held in great abhorrence by the Brahmins, and who cordially detest each other. They do not admit their connexion with Buddhism, and they are only identified with it by similar customs and ceremonies, and by their acknowledgment of the same faith which has obtained in Thibet and Pegu. They agree with the Brahmins in their adoration of the Ganges, and their respect for Benares; but they declare, that although others may be acquainted with the true God, they alone know how to worship him. Jain temples are to be found in several parts of India, but, like the Brahmins, they have deserted those of Ellora. The Jains are not a very extensive community, but many belonging to the sect have attained considerable wealth in mercantile pursuits.

The obelisks of Kylas, one of which is visible in the accompanying engraving, the upper part arising above the outer scarp of the rock, are objects of great interest and curiosity. They are ornaments placed in front of the area between the temple and the gateway, and on either side of the chapel, if it may be so called, dedicated to the bull Nundi. These obelisks are of a quadrangular form, eleven feet square, sculptured in a great variety of devices, which are distinguished by the beauty of their finish: their height is about forty-one feet, and they were surmounted by the effigy of some animal, supposed to be a lion, which, though not an object of Brahminical veneration, occurs very frequently in the sculptures throughout the cave temples. In a preceding view of Kylas, there is a representation of one of these obelisks, which would in itself be worthy of a visit from all the savans of Europe, were it not surrounded by objects still more wonderful. It is larger at the base than Cleopatra's needle in Egypt, and, as well as the remainder of the temple, belonged to the solid rock, being hewn out of the hill when Kylas, which, unlike the other cave excavations, is insulated, without the ponderous living roof which rises over the rest of the caves, was first projected. Kylas is also distinguished for the splendour of its upper story, the ascent is by two flights of stairs, one on each side of the principal excavation, consisting of thirty-six steps, winding inwards, which lead to the top of the portico of the temple, and conduct the visitor across a bridge to the apartments over the gateway, which appear in the annexed plate. The remains of a lion are seen on the top of the portico and in the interior there are two figures, pronounced to be sphynxes, the only place in which these emblems occur throughout the whole range of the hill. Sphynxes, it is said, are found in the Bhoodhist temples of Ava, and Sir Stamford Raffles fancied that he had discovered one in Java, but those in India have been subjects of great speculation and dispute. The bridge, so often mentioned, leading to the balcony over the gateway, is furnished with a parapet, three feet six inches in height; and from the balcony itself, the eye ranges over one of the most pleasing views which imagination can portray. The hill sweeps down for about half a mile from the excavations in gradual descent to the plain, which is of considerable magnitude, but relieved by scattered groups of trees, and the village of Ellora arising in the distance.

The temple of Kylas is still much frequented by faquirs, religious mendicants, who, however, are to be found wherever there is a spot which has once been esteemed holy. It is necessary for visitors who wish to spend sufficient time amidst the excavations, to make themselves acquainted with the numerous objects of curiosity which they contain, to conciliate these people, who are fond of appearing to be of consequence, and lose no opportunity of shewing that they will not suffer themselves or their religion to be treated with any kind of disrespect. In their character of holy men, it would be unsafe as well as unwise to give them just cause of provocation, but it is not difficult to secure their good will. A few rupees, or a present of grain, accompanied by courteous words and a disposition to respect their religious prejudices, will be invariably successful amid all classes of Hindoos, who, though not of that mild and peaceable temperament which has been so generally attributed to the worshippers of the cow, are easily subdued by kindness. A liberal, or even a just person, who possesses gracious manners, may make his way all over India with the greatest facility; no temple will be closed against him, and no privilege, which it is possible to grant, withheld. Unfortunately, the English are not conspicuous for the suavity of their manners, or for their toleration of foreign creeds and customs; and there is some danger, in throwing open India to all sorts of adventurers, of creating a disgust amongst the natives which may occasion the loss of our empire in the East. The introduction of beef by the visitors at Ellora would, even now, be attended with serious consequences. Persons lately arrived in the country, who have had no opportunity of making themselves acquainted with the extreme horror which the Hindoos, in many parts of India, entertain at the bare idea of the slaughter of the sacred animal, are too apt to treat so ridiculous a prejudice with contempt, though there is nothing more likely to create a serious disturbance than the sacrifice of an ox in any spot esteemed holy.

THE CAVE OF KARLI.

CAVE OF KARLI.

This celebrated excavation, like all the cave temples of India, stands upon Mahratta ground. It occurs in the province of Arungabad, in the midst of a chain of hills running east and west, of a very picturesque character. Many of the ridges are level, but others tower above in lonely majesty, lifting their summits high into the heavens. Most of these eminences, however, have platforms of table land at the top, and are, on that account, admirably calculated for the hill-fortresses which were such favourite places of defence in the early ages of Indian warfare: two of these mountain citadels arise in the vicinity of Karli; they are merely separated by a valley, and their scarped sides and bastioned heights give them a very formidable appearance.

The entrance of the cave of Karli, or Ekverah, forms the subject of the accompanying plate. It is situated at the distance of about three hundred feet from the base of the hill, and is approached by a very toilsome pathway, which has more the appearance of a water-course than a regular road, being very steep, and exceedingly rugged. This track leads to a terrace or platform, partly artificial, being cut into the hill, and constructed of the rock hewn out of the interior. It is about a hundred feet wide, and forms an appropriate approach to the magnificent temple within. In front, and on the left side of the entrance, there is a column twenty-four feet high, and about eight in diameter; the upper part is dome-shaped, surmounted by a flat slab, on which are the remains of three lions, much injured by time's decaying hand. It is supposed that a corresponding pillar on the opposite side has been removed to make room for the small temple which appears there dedicated to the goddess Bowannee, a deity in high favour with Hindoos of the Brahminical persuasion. The column is decorated with an inscription in a character which has hitherto baffled every attempt made to decipher it.

A screen originally ran across the entrance, but this has been partly broken down, and displays the grandeur of the arch which is cut over the door-way, an aperture certainly not commensurate with the noble dimensions of the interior. Between the outer and inner screens there is a veranda, or vestibule, extending the whole length of the cave, very finely sculptured with figures of men and animals in alto relievo. Three colossal elephants stand on each side, with drivers on their necks, and riders in their howdahs, executed in a very free and bold manner; and other figures, both male and female, are finished in the same animated style. The sculptures of deities at Karli are confined to the walls, the only peculiar object of worship being a large circular altar of stone, surmounted by a wooden canopy. The length of the great cavern is one hundred and twenty-six feet, and it is forty-six feet wide. The roof, which is arched and ribbed with wood, a circumstance which injures its effect, is supported by two rows of pillars, each surmounted by an elephant, bearing a male and female figure on its back, encircling each other in their arms, and crouching beneath the weight above them.

The interior of the temple is very grand and imposing, but it is more gloomy than any of the other excavations noticed in the present work. Some persons are of opinion that

Karli was formerly illuminated, as, without the aid of lamps or torches, the figures in the side-aisles are not distinguishable, and the pains taken to sculpture them would have been thrown away; but India furnishes so many instances of an utter disregard to consequences, that some more conclusive evidence is necessary to decide the point. The wood work is supposed to have been added to Karli at a period subsequent to its first formation; it is teak, and is said to have lasted nine hundred years; a part of this ribbing may be seen upon the roof of the arch in front, and the high state of its preservation shews the great durability of a species of timber which has rivalled oak in the building of ships.

The learned have decided Karli to be a Bhoodhist temple, the figure of Bhood, and the symbols attached to it, being the predominant ornaments, while it is destitute of a single vestige of the twenty-four saints of the Jains, a distinguishing feature in the temples belonging to that sect. There are other apartments besides the great cavern; but these are in a rude unfinished state, and present nothing worthy of notice. Outside the cavern there are a few native huts, inhabited by the servants of the Brahmins, who are, or rather were, a few years ago, in greater force at Karli than at any other of the cave temples. One of these holy persons might, from his indifference to worldly concerns, and total abandonment to religious contemplation, have been taken for an image of Bhood himself. He sat night and day before a flame of fire, with a cloth over his mouth to prevent him from inhaling pollution, and he subsisted solely upon parched grain, and water strained through a cloth. The peishwa, who had endeavoured vainly to induce this self-denying being to reside at his court, supported him and his associates from his own treasury; and doubtless the fraternity will be kept up, for vacancies by death, of ascetics in India, are immediately filled, many being ambitious of succeeding to the hermitages of holy men, even though they should be exposed to the most imminent danger from the attacks of wild beasts.

The view from the terrace outside the temple is very fine, stretching over a rich and beautiful country, bounded by a chain of distant mountains. The village of Karli, about two miles and a quarter from the excavations, forms a pretty object in the landscape; its rural habitations peep out from the midst of mango groves, and it is further embellished by a large tank, and a pagoda of very considerable architectural beauty. The chain of mountains amid which these excavations are placed extend from Cape Comorin, in a series unbroken, except at one place about twelve miles broad in the Malabar territory northward to the province of Candeish. This hilly district never recedes more than fifty miles from the sea, or approaches within eight. There are not many passes known to Europeans, and formerly the passage of the ghauts was a service of great difficulty and danger; and even now these hills do not appear to have so strongly attracted the attention of scientific travellers as their mineral wealth would lead us to suppose. That so many interesting scenes, occurring in territories belonging to the British government, should have remained a terra incognita during such a lengthened period as that in which we have occupied Bombay and its adjacencies, seems exceedingly surprising. India, less fortunate than South America, has had no Humboldt to investigate its numerous sources of scientific interest; and should the researches of M. Jacquemont meet the public eye,

AKBAR'S TOMB.—SECUNDRA.

the French nation will have the honour of giving to the world information upon a subject which has been most unaccountably neglected by those who have left one of the richest harvests in the world to be gathered by foreigners.

Nothing can exceed the natural strength of the country within the western ghauts: though called table land, it is finely diversified by hill and dale, and in some parts may even be styled mountainous; much of the rock is covered with a very rich mould, and instead of presenting the bare, rugged, sterile peaks which distinguish the eastern chain, they are clothed with luxuriant forests to their summits. In no part of India is there finer timber, and the bamboos are superior in size and strength to those which grow in less luxuriant soils. The rattan also attains a gigantic height, and the most sublime and splendid views imaginable are obtained from many points of the different passes. In addition to their botanical, mineralogical, and geological treasures, and the magnificent excavations which are contained within their limits, the western ghauts afford very curious meteorological data, the range to the southward being sufficiently lofty to intercept the progress of the clouds, and to occasion an extraordinary difference of climate on the windward side.

AKBAR'S TOMB—SECUNDRA.

Amidst the numerous monumental remains of the Moghul conquerors of India, the magnificent pile which heaps terrace upon terrace over the ashes of the mighty Akbar, if not the most chaste and beautiful in its design, is certainly the most spacious and splendid which Hindoostan can boast. This superb mausoleum stands in the centre of a park-like plantation of not less than forty acres in extent, the whole area being surrounded by a battlemented wall, strengthened by an octagonal tower at each corner. These towers are built in a very noble style, and are crowned with an open cupola at the top. There are also four gateways handsomely constructed of red granite; but three of these entrances are eclipsed by the superior splendour of the fourth, which is one of the most magnificent edifices of the kind to be found in India. It has often fallen to our lot to expatiate upon the majestic approaches which the vast conceptions of an Indian architect include in the designs for palace, tomb, or mosque. The outer entrance is always in keeping with the principal building arresting the gaze of the visitor, who can scarcely imagine that any thing more beautiful is to be seen beyond. The gate at Secundra, with its spacious arched gothic hall and lofty marble minarets, would in itself be considered worthy to commemorate the deeds of the most renowned warrior of the world; and we linger at the portal, notwithstanding the temptation to hurry onwards to the spot where the mighty Akbar lies entombed.

The annexed plate gives a very correct representation of a building exceedingly singular in its design, and differing widely from the usual features of Moghul architecture. It forms a perfect square; the basement story containing nothing worthy of note excepting its outer colonnade—the four passages leading from the four gateways—and the dim vault in which the body of Akbar, enclosed in a marble sarcophagus, reposes.

A lamp is burning on the tomb, daily fed by the pious care of a few poor brethren of the Moosulman priesthood, who also strew fresh flowers over the unconscious dead; a beautiful custom, prevalent in every part of Hindoostan. Above this chamber there is a second, a third, and a fourth, each forming a distinct story, and rising directly over the body, and each containing a marble sarcophagus; but there are no large halls, no spacious apartments, and the rooms, which are entered from the cloistered verandas of the terraces, are exceedingly small, and may almost be denominated cells. Flights of stairs lead from the entrances below to the first platform, the building being in the form of a pyramid with its apex cut off. This story consists of four noble terraces, or rather one quadrangle, with the central chamber before mentioned; its suites of small apartments, and cloistered arcade in the midst, presenting the same façade on every side. The whole is surrounded by a noble balustrade, and at each angle there is a large pavilion-like turret with an open cupola. Flights of stairs lead to the second terraced quadrangle, which is precisely the same as the lower one, except that it is smaller, and each tier diminishes in size until we reach the summit of the building, and enter upon a large marble platform, surrounded on the four sides by a screen of white marble, perforated in every compartment in beautiful patterns of arabesques, and having turreted marble cupolas at the angles. In the centre stands a fifth sarcophagus; this is most delicately and beautifully carved, the name of the monarch who sleeps below being inscribed upon it in gems. Though exposed to every change of atmosphere, its beauty remains unimpaired by the sunny climate of the East, and, notwithstanding the lapse of years, it is still as pure, as white, and as brilliantly polished as ever. The three stories which intervene between this roofless chamber and the basement floor are constructed of red granite, fantastically inlaid with white marble. The cupolas are covered with coloured tiles composed of a coarse description of enamel; and altogether there is more of barbaric pomp displayed in this mausoleum than is usually to be found in the elegant and tasteful edifices which the Mohammedans of India have reared to the memory of departed greatness.

While the upper part of the building may form a legitimate subject for criticism, nothing can be finer than the gateways and the wide marble colonnades which sweep along each side of the tomb. These spacious cloisters would afford accommodation for a large army; the regiment of English dragoons which was quartered in them during the siege of Agra under Lord Lake, occupied but a small portion: they lead to marble chambers screened off from each other, in which several members of the imperial family are enshrined, and they are flanked with solid towers, their cupola'd summits forming pavilions to the terrace above. The interior of the arch at the principal entrance, the one to the right in the accompanying plate, is embellished with verses which commemorate the fame, virtues, and triumphs of the founder, and expatiate upon the instability of human grandeur.

From every terrace of this magnificent building, a splendid view of the adjacent country is gained. The first looks down upon luxuriant plantations of umbrageous trees, where the lofty tamarind forms a glorious back-ground to the citron and orange, rich in flower and in fruit; picturesque groups of cattle give life and animation to a scene, which, shewing touches of decay in prostrate columns, and causeways suffering from the want of repair, is somewhat of a melancholy character. From the second terrace, a wider extent of landscape presents itself—cultivated plains splendidly wooded, and interspersed with innumerable buildings, whose dilapidated state is concealed by distance, while the topmost height commands one of the finest prospects in the world; the Jumna winding like a silvery snake through fertile tracts, luxuriant in foliage, and wealthy in the richest specimens of architecture; palaces and villas, the imperial city and turreted walls of the fort of Agra, with the Mootee Musjid (pearl-mosque) rearing its glittering cupolas on high; and, beyond, closing the magnificent perspective, the snow-white dome and slender minars of the Taj Mahal, catching the golden light of a cloudless sun.

The tomb of Akbar is situated about seven miles from Agra, which is supposed in the days of its glory to have extended to the very gates of the surrounding enclosure. Now the visitors wend their way through a picturesque country strewed with ruins, and along the streets of a second-rate but bustling commercial town, situated midway between the city and the tomb, to the village of Secundra, a place which bears the marks of former opulence and greatness, but which now only affords a shelter to a few of the poorest peasants, content to dwell beneath the crumbling roofs of decaying grandeur.

The neighbouring inhabitants, notwithstanding the pride they take in the name of Akbar, plume themselves upon occupying ground rendered illustrious by a still more distinguished conqueror. They shew the figure of a horse, not badly sculptured in red stone, which they call Bucephalus; and they boast that their village derives its appellation from the great Secundra, Alexander of Macedon—a name which all over India, both Moslem and Hindoo, pronounce with reverence and respect. Probably one of the successors to a fragment of the heroic madman's gigantic empire extended his conquests beyond the Indus, and left behind him records of valour which are now attributed to Philip's warlike son. The natives, who cherish an extraordinary veneration for the dead, are happy in the supposition that they possess the ashes of this mighty conqueror, whose reputed tomb on the summit of the hill at Secunder Mallee, in the Carnatic, is said to be guarded by royal tigers, who keep the platform clean by sweeping it with their tails. The virtues of Akbar's private character, his long and glorious reign, and the stability which his invariable success gave to an empire which had so nearly fallen a second time under the dominion of the Afghauns, have inspired the people of Hindoostan with the highest regard for his memory. The eyes of the natives sparkle as they utter his name, and the faithful though indigent few, who now supply the places of the glittering courtiers offering flattering incense to the living emperor, warmly express their delight when pilgrims from far and foreign lands come to pay homage at his lonely sepulchre. The mausoleum itself is kept in tolerable repair by the government, but an air of desolation is spread over the surrounding buildings. The great gateway belonging to the outer wall is in so dangerous a state, that visitors are afraid to venture under its trembling walls; large stones detached from the main edifice are continually falling, and a breach in the neighbouring wall, another symptom of neglect, affords a safer entrance. The renown so justly linked with the name of the great Akbar is of so absorbing a character, that few of the visitors to his splendid shrine bestow more than a passing glance at the recesses, not very unlike Roman Catholic chapels attached to some great cathedral, where the less distinguished scions of his house repose. One of these is particularly interesting, from its containing the ashes of a Hindoo princess, induced by political considerations to give up her kindred and caste, and become the wife of a foreign conqueror differing from herself in colour and in creed. The Moghuls of that period still retained the fairness of complexion upon which at the present day they pride themselves, though with little justice, since frequent intermarriages with the children of the soil have deepened the tint of their skins to the same swarthy hue. Throughout the whole course of Mohammedan invasion, the most determined hostility to unions of this nature has been manifested by the unbending Hindoo: many thousand females have been sacrificed by their fathers and brothers, rather than they should fall into the hands of the profane conquerors who desecrated their altars with the blood of bulls; nevertheless, individual instances occurred, in which the concession was considered too essential to be withheld, and the daughters of Rajpoots have been found in the palaces of the Moghul.

CHINESE JUNK,—CANTON RIVER.

Voyagers accustomed to the scientific improvements in ship-building which characterize the present era, are struck with amazement when they encounter for the first time, amongst the islands of the Indian ocean, the clumsy, ill-contrived vessels which still continue to be navigated by the Chinese. The description given of the large trading junks at present in use amongst this singular people, by Barrow, in his Travels in China, is the best and most perfect which is extant, and, though quoted before, must be preferred to any less authentic account. After stating that these ships, in consequence of the peculiarity of their construction, appear to be very unfit to contend with the tempestuous seas of China, he make sthe following observations :—" The general form of the hull above water, is that of the moon when about four days old. The bow is not rounded, as in the ships of Europe, but is a square flat surface, the same as the stern, without any projecting piece of wood, usually known by the name of cutwater, and the vessel is without any keel; on each side of the bow a large circular eye is painted; the two ends of the ship rise to a prodigious height above the deck; some carry two, others three, and some four masts, and each of these consist of single pieces of wood, consequently they are incapable of being reduced in length occasionally, as those of European ships. The diameter of the mainmast of one of the larger kinds of Chinese vessels, such as trade to Batavia, is equal to that of an English ship of war of sixty guns, and it is fixed in a bed of massive timber laid across the deck; on each mast is a single sail of matting made from the fibres of the bamboo, and stretched by means of poles of that reed, running across at intervals of about two feet from top to bottom. These sails are made to furl and unfurl like a fan. When well hoisted up, and braced almost fore and aft, a Chinese vessel will lie within three and a half or four points of the wind; but they lose this advantage over

A CHINESE JUNK.—CANTON RIVER.

ships of Europe, by their drifting to leeward in consequence of the round, clumsy shape of the bottom, and their want of keel." Captain R. Elliot, in quoting this passage, observes, that " a square-rigged vessel, as ships are commonly called in England, is not considered to come nearer the wind than six points, with any benefit, in going to windward." The same author, in noticing Mr. Barrow's statement, of the rudder being so placed in a large aperture in the stern as to admit of its being occasionally taken up, draws the attention of the reader to the annexed plate, where the rudder seems to be triced up, apparently to make room for the cables; and he also gives some curious information respecting the internal construction of these vessels. The hold of the ship is divided into many compartments, made water-tight like the bottom, there being sometimes as many as sixty of these warerooms in a large vessel; they have no communication, excepting with the well in the centre; wherefore, if the ship should spring a leak in any one of these chambers, and it should not be found possible to reduce the water, that cavity alone would fill, and the buoyancy of the vessel would not be materially affected.

The Chinese are little skilled in the art of navigation. It is now proved beyond a doubt, that they were in possession of the compass long before it was known in Europe; but they have no other instruments worthy of notice, and it is very problematical whether they were ever guided by a chart. Yet, in despite of the ignorance which the mariners of the Celestial Empire manifested concerning latitude and longitude, their want of acquaintance with the heavenly bodies, and the dangerous tempests which frequently agitate the ocean, they seem to have always put to sea with great confidence, carrying their trade as far as Batavia, and even to more distant places.

The internal commerce of China is very considerable; and from Canton, which is one of the great emporia of the empire, the products of distant provinces find their way to every part of the globe. Kwang-tung sends to the metropolis silks, rice, fish, salt, fruits, vegetables, and various kinds of wood, silver, iron, and pearls in small quantities, cassia, and betel nuts. From Fah-keen come the black teas; also camphor, sugar, indigo, tobacco, paper, lacquered ware, excellent grass cloth, and a few mineral productions; woollen and cotton cloths of various kinds; wines and watches are sent in return to this province. Che-heang sends to Canton the best of silks and paper; also fans, pencils, wines, dates, golden-flowered brocades, and lung-ting-cha, an excellent and very costly tea. There are likewise, from other provinces, fruits, drugs, dates, skins, and deers' flesh, gold, brass, iron, tin, musk, feathers, quicksilver, birds, precious stones, honey, hemp, indigo, and china-ware.

The junks trading to Batavia are laden with cargoes of teas, raw silk, piece goods, varnished umbrellas, iron pots, coarse chinaware, sweetmeats, nankeen, paper, and many minor articles. They also carry out considerable numbers of emigrants: for, though the Chinese government does not sanction the departure of its subjects as settlers in foreign countries, numbers are to be found living under the protection of the authorities in all the European colonies of the East. A whole street in Calcutta, named the Cossitollah, is chiefly tenanted by Chinese shoemakers, a frugal, industrious race, who sometimes acquire very large fortunes, which in few cases, if they return to their own country, are they permitted to enjoy in peace. A hakeem, or doctor, has accompanied them to the Bengal presidency, who, notwithstanding the profound ignorance of the science which distinguishes the professors of the healing art in China, and the ease with which the best medical aid is procurable in Calcutta, carries on an extensive practice, and may be seen every evening on the public drive, seated in an European chariot, which, though not quite so magnificent as some which figure on the hackney-coach stands in London, nevertheless forms a most respectable equipage in Bengal. Chinese natives emigrating to the islands, succeed even better than those who have to cope with the thrift-loving Hindoos of the continent; and the residents of Batavia carry on a very considerable trade with the mother country in birds' nests. Malayan camphor *bich de mar*, tin, opium, pepper, timber, leather, hides, gold, and silver.

CHANDGOAN.

The temple represented in the accompanying engraving forms one of the numerous edifices of the same nature which occur in lonely and unfrequented parts of India, and appearing as if merely formed to cheer the eye of the traveller as he journeys along an almost depopulated wilderness. The adjacent village to which this large and handsome pagoda belongs is so small and insignificant, as not to be mentioned in any map or guide-book hitherto extant. It is situated in the south-eastern quarter of the Jeypore territory, and lies in the route from Agra to Kota, and other places in Central India. Chandgoan occurs in the middle of a stage, and therefore it is only from some accident that travellers halt in its neighbourhood, or obtain more than a casual glance at the pagoda as they march along. The country round about is not by any means interesting, consisting of one of those flat arid plains thinly clothed with scattered trees, which so often fatigue the eye during a journey through the upper provinces of Hindoostan.

The temple is very picturesque, and affords a good specimen of Hindoo architecture, unmixed by foreign importations; the pointed mitre-like figure of the cupolas shew the antiquity of the structure, the greater number of Hindoo buildings erected after the settlement of the Mohammedans in the country having the round domes introduced by the conquerors. The shrines of the deities are placed in these steeple-crowned temples; the part devoted to religious worship of a large pagoda frequently not bearing any proportion to that which is intended for the accommodation of the officiating Brahmins and their various attendants. A troop of dancing-girls are often domesticated within the precincts of some well-endowed temple; they are not the most immaculate of their sex, but their devotion to the service of the god sanctifies their occupation, and the Nautch women belonging to a pagoda are never considered to be so degraded and impure as those who have not the honour to live under Brahminical protection. Poor persons feel no objection to devote their daughters to this kind of life; and deserted children, who are taken out of compassion by the Brahmins, are always brought up to assist at the religious festivals, which are frequently accompanied by theatrical exhibitions. There is one especially, in honour of Krishna, in which, after the dancing-girls have displayed their art,

HINDOO TEMPLE AT CHANDNGOAN.

Views in

I N D I A

China, and on the Shores of the Red Sea

VOL. II.

BABOO Kasiprasad Ghosh

a ballet is performed by young boys educated for the purpose, who represent the early adventures of the deity during his sojourn in the nether world. These boys are always Brahmins, and the most accomplished belong to Muttra, a place scarcely inferior to Benares in sanctity. The corps de ballet, if they may be so denominated, attached to any Hindoo establishment of great celebrity, travel about during the seasons of particular festivals, and perform at the different courts of Hindoo princes. They are always extremely well paid for their exertions, and become a source of wealth to the pagoda to which they belong. This explanation will account for the numerous suites of apartments intended for human inhabitants, which are usually to be found within the enclosures of the sacred buildings of the Hindoos.

Little or nothing is at present known concerning Chandgoan, though by its perfect condition it appears to have funds for its repair at its disposal. Placed upon the borders of Jeypore, it is not in the neighbourhood of any city of note; and though the province is now under British protection, it is rarely visited by the Anglo-Indian residents of Hindoostan. The capital of the state, which is one of the most splendid cities of the peninsula, and certainly the finest belonging to Rajpootana, attracts comparatively a very small portion of attention. With the exception of the notice in Hamilton's Gazetteer, a work which is not so universally read as it deserves to be, little or nothing was known of this city until the publication of Bishop Heber's Journal, and the learned prelate seems to have been wholly unprepared for the magnificence of its architecture.

BABOO KASIPRASAD GHOSH.

The subject of this interesting portrait is a young Hindoo of family and fortune, of brahminical descent, belonging to the Kayartha caste, or, as it is called in the upper provinces of Hindoostan, kayst. His ancestors, who were natives of Kanoge, were invited by a prince of Bengal to settle in his territories, and to aid him in the administration of his government. Since the period of British ascendance, the family of Kasiprasad Ghosh have lived as private gentlemen; the term Baboo, prefixed to his name, being equivalent with that of Esquire. At the age of fourteen, the young Hindoo was sent to complete his education at the Anglo-Indian college at Calcutta, at that time under the able superintendence of Horace Hayman Wilson, Esq., now Sanscrit professor at Oxford. He remained six years at his studies, and during the last three carried away all the honours. At a public examination in 1827, for which, in compliance with Mr. Wilson's desire, he had prepared a paper entitled "Critical Remarks upon the British India of Mr. Mill," he was greatly distinguished; and part of the essay being printed in the government gazette of Calcutta, it was deemed worthy of republication in the Asiatic Journal. Enthusiastically devoted to the study of English literature, soon after this period Kasiprasad Ghosh became a contributor to the Calcutta periodicals; he composed verses in Bengalee, but the greater portion of his writings were in English, in which he expressed himself with so much strength, grace, and facility, as justly to excite the surprise and admiration of all who could judge of the great difficulties to be encountered in composing poetry in a foreign language. The praise and encouragement which were very liberally bestowed upon the youthful poet's efforts by the Calcutta press, led to the publication of a volume entitled "The Shair," the Hindoostanee word for Minstrel. This work established the author's reputation as a poet in India, and has been very favourably noticed in England. Independent of the extraordinary circumstances under which it was produced, the numerous obstacles which a native of a foreign and a distant land, whose creed, manners, customs, habits, and modes of thinking, differ so widely from our own, must encounter in entering the lists with English poets, the Shair possesses merits which would always entitle it to consideration. The limited space to which a notice of each plate in these volumes must necessarily be confined, will not permit a more detailed examination of the various claims which Kasiprasad Ghosh possesses to the attention of the English reader. The fervid Orientalisms of a little poem, entitled "The Boatman's Song to Ganga," have rendered it a favourite with those who have had an opportunity of quoting the works of the young Hindoo. It is perhaps the most beautiful of any of the productions from the same pen; but as it has already appeared in two of the annuals of the present year, the following lines from the introduction to the third canto of the Shair, may be preferred, as being less known.

" 'Tis evening—to the western heaven,
His golden car the sun has driven;
And to the Ganges' waters bright,
Weary directs his homeward flight.
Hail, brightest ornament of day!
Resplendent gem of ruby ray!
How rich with many a glittering hue,
Of gold and purple, red and blue,
Yon flaming orb of heaven doth shine,
Made by thy parting ray divine!
How bright beneath thy various beam,
Wanders the sacred Ganges' stream!
But, lo! beneath the waters now,
To rest from labour sinkest thou.
Bereft of thee, so famed in lays,
The lotus of the ancient days,
Upon the holy wave behold,
Begins its petals now to fold.
The pale hue of dejectedness
Its drooping head doth now express;
And darkness growing in the rear,
Bereft of thee doth eve appear;
As if, in widowhood's despair,
A maiden rushed with loosened hair."

THE BRITISH RESIDENCY AT HYDERABAD.

THE BRITISH RESIDENCY AT HYDERABAD.

The splendid building represented in the accompanying plate, was erected for the accommodation of the British resident, by the Nizam of Hyderabad, a native Mohammedan prince, who is sovereign of a very considerable territory. The original plan was made, and the whole of the execution superintended, by a young officer of the Madras Engineers, a branch of the service which furnishes the architects of the European community in India. The façade shewn in the engraving is the south, or back front, looking towards the city, from which it is separated by the river Moosy. The front towards the north is erected in a corresponding style of elegance, being adorned with a spacious Corinthian portico of six columns. The house to the right, standing immediately above the bank of the river, is occupied by the officer commanding the Resident's escort; and the whole, with its fine accompaniments of wood and water, affords a magnificent and striking scene, scarcely less imposing than that which is presented by the Government House at Calcutta. The artist has taken advantage of the frequent visits of ceremony passing between the Nizam and the Resident, to introduce one of those picturesque cavalcades which form the most splendid pageants of the East. The covered Ambarry, a vehicle usually of silver or gold, canopied with gold brocade, which surmounts the back of the foremost elephant, is an emblem of royalty, none save sovereign princes being permitted to use an equipage of this description. The second elephant bears the common native howdah, which is often formed of solid silver, or of wood covered with silver plates, and is the conveyance employed by noblemen and gentlemen of rank. There is room in front for two persons, and a seat behind for an attendant, who, upon ordinary occasions, carries an umbrella, but in the presence of monarchy no person of inferior rank is permitted to interpose any screen between the sun and his devoted head. The British Resident, as the representative of his Sovereign, has a right to a seat in the Ambarry; and it is the etiquette upon great occasions, for the prince who desires to testify his respect for the government with which he is in friendly alliance, to invite the party whom he wishes to honour, to share his own elephant.

Hyderabad gives its name to a large province in the Deccan, between the sixteenth and nineteenth degrees of north latitude. It was invaded and subjugated at an early period of the Mohammedan conquests in India, and formed afterwards a portion of the great Bhamanee empire of the Deccan. Though Aurungzebe succeeded in reducing all the Moslem princes who had established themselves in Hindostan, Hyderabad did not very long remain a dependent state. The soubadahs, appointed to govern it, soon threw off their allegiance, and, upon the destruction of the Moghul empire, the Nizam, one of the titles assumed by the reigning prince, became a personage of considerable importance in the Deccan, and, by the assistance of the British government, was enabled to maintain his territory in despite of the utmost efforts made by the Mahrattas to wrest it from him. Though it is more than suspected that the Nizam was secretly favourable to the project formed by the native chieftains, who, under the guidance of the Peishwa, threw down the gauntlet, and attempted to dispossess the British of their dominions in the East, no open rupture ensued, and the two powers have always maintained an outward semblance of friendship. The court of Hyderabad is kept up with great splendour, and there is more of the ancient ceremonial retained than is usual in the present depressed condition of native princes. The Omrahs are men of considerable wealth, and there is a constant and increasing demand for foreign luxuries at the capital.